LONGMAN IMPRINT BOOKS

Travel Writing

Major writers travel the world

Selected and edited by Linda Marsh

General editor: Michael Marland
Series consultant: Geoff Barton

LONGMAN

Post-1914 Stories from other Cultures

Angelou, Goodison, Senior & Walker **Quartet of Stories** 0 582 28730 8
Nadine Gordimer **July's People** 0 582 06011 7
Ruth Prawer Jhabvala **Heat and Dust** 0 582 25398 5
Alan Paton **Cry, the Beloved Country** 0 582 07787 7
selected by Madhu Bhinda **Stories from Africa** 0 582 25393 4
Stories from Asia 0 582 03922 3
selected by B Naidoo, C Donovan, A Hicks **Global Tales** 0 582 28929 7

Post-1914 Non-Fiction

selected by Geoff Barton **Genres** 0 582 25391 8
selected by Celeste Flower **Diaries and Letters** 0 582 25384 5
selected by Peter Griffiths **Introducing Media** 0 582 28932 7
selected by Linda Marsh **Travel Writing** 0 582 25386 1
Autobiographies 0 582 08837 2

The Diary of Anne Frank 0 582 01736 X

Pre-1914 Fiction

Jane Austen **Pride and Prejudice** 0 582 07720 6
Charlotte Brontë **Jane Eyre** 0 582 07719 2
Emily Brontë **Wuthering Heights** 0 582 07782 6
Charles Dickens **Great Expectations** 0 582 07783 4
Oliver Twist 0 582 28729 4
A Christmas Carol 0 582 23664 9
George Eliot **Silas Marner** 0 582 23662 2
Thomas Hardy **The Mayor of Casterbridge** 0 582 22586 8
Far from the Madding Crowd 0 582 07788 5

Pre-1914 Collections

Thomas Hardy **Wessex Tales** 0 582 25405 1
selected by Geoff Barton **Two Centuries** 0 582 25390 X
Stories Old and New 0 582 28931 9
selected by Jane Christopher **War Stories** 0 582 28927 0
selected by Susie Campbell **Characters from Pre-20th Century Novels** 0 582 25388 8
selected by Celeste Flower **Diaries and Letters** 0 582 25384 5
selected by Linda Marsh **Highlights from 19th-Century Novels** 0 582 25385 3
Landmarks 0 582 25389 6
Travel Writing 0 582 25386 1
selected by Tony Parkinson **Nineteenth-Century Short Stories of Passion and Mystery**
0 582 33807 7

Pre-1914 Poetry

edited by Adrian Tissier **Poems from Other Centuries** 0 582 22585 X

Pre-1914 Plays

Oliver Goldsmith **She Stoops to Conquer** 0 582 25397 7
Henrik Ibsen **Three Plays** 0 582 24948 1
Christopher Marlowe **Doctor Faustus** 0 582 25409 4
selected by Linda Marsh **Starting Shakespeare** 0 582 28930 0
Bernard Shaw **The Devil's Disciple** 0 582 25410 8
Arms and the Man 0 582 07785 0
John Webster **The Duchess of Malfi** 0 582 28731 6
Oscar Wilde **The Importance of Being Earnest** 0 582 07784 2

Contents

Introduction

In June 1930, two men squeezed through a little round hole into a steel ball measuring just under one and a half metres in diameter. Steel bolts and huge nuts fastened the door on, and down they went, dropping three times the depth to which any human being had ever penetrated the ocean. 'A quarter of a mile down,' said Dr Beebe into the telephone, 'and we're still alive.' A loosening of the pressure, and the first drops of water would shoot through them like bullets.

They did survive, and went on to try again, going deeper still. 'No pioneer, peering at a Martian landscape, could ever have a greater thrill than I did at such an opportunity,' Dr Beebe concluded.

Such a distance into the sea was as death-defying, as remarkable then, as the later voyages into space. The same sense of wonder experienced by those doctors and scientists can be glimpsed in Fanny Kemble's experience of her trip on the first train, pulled by Stephenson's *Rocket*, in 1830. The 'snorting little animal' was attached to their carriage and they started off at 10 m.p.h. They 'came to a moss, or swamp . . . on which no human foot could tread without sinking, and yet it bore the road which bore us.' At 35 m.p.h. 'You cannot conceive what that sensation of cutting the air was.'

Some writers have described smaller journeys with equal feeling. 'The worst journey of my life,' writes William Trevor, 'involved neither hardship, pain nor danger. It was not particularly uncomfortable. I suffered neither undue hunger nor thirst, extremes of neither heat nor cold. What possessed me was dread, and the misery of anticipating the unavoidable. I was twelve years old on the morning of April 28th 1941. I was returning to boarding school, and I knew what awaited me.'

The travellers in this collection narrate just such journeys of excitement, of fears and discoveries. They explore places for which there are no maps, or they visit well-known places and bring them to us freshly. Many are brave, resourceful and inspired. Sometimes they go on – what Freya Stark would call – 'journeys of the heart', or they conjure up a 'spirit of place' and make you long to go there.

Kenneth Grahame in *The Wind in the Willows* described the pull of homecomings too. 'Mole's little front door, with "Mole End" painted, in Gothic lettering, over the bell-pull at the side,' shows us 'the special value of some such anchorage in one's existence. He did not at all want to abandon the new life and its splendid spaces . . . But it was good to think he had this to come back to, this place which was all his own.'

All travellers start from somewhere. Perhaps this book will help to open up the world for you, and it may also give you a deeper sense of home.

Linda Marsh

Lift-Off!

from *Seize the Moment*

by Helen Sharman

Helen Sharman has been chosen to join a Soviet team as the first British astronaut and, after a long period of intense training, is now ready for her first voyage into space. She and her two fellow-astronauts are now driving towards the launch pad, and the rocket is straight ahead.

It was the first time I had been able to get a good, uninterrupted look at it. Nothing in training can prepare you for the prospect of your own rocket, the real one, the actual one that is going to start its engines and lift you away from the Earth. There was ours. It was grey and solid against the neutral sky, the three main supporting gantries by now tipped back on their counterweights. All that remained were the four small launch-gantries clustered around the base and the tower with the elevator that would lift us to the capsule. White condensation poured off the rocket, seeming to roll down its flanks, a momentary slow-motion illusion of the upward rush for which it had been built. The rocket was a little smaller than perhaps I had expected, but there was something so purposeful, almost heroic, about its utilitarian lines that I could only stare at it in awe. I felt a tremendous sense of respect for it, as if it were, itself, alive.

Close to the top, on the white-painted fairing that surrounded the capsule inside which I would soon be seated, they had painted two flags: the Soviet flag and, for the first time in manned space travel, the Union Jack.

The bus came to a halt at the base of the rocket and the three of us climbed down first. Most of the people who had been with us stayed on the bus, staring out at us silently through the windows. On the pad some of the technicians waved and cheered. We walked the short distance to the metal steps, right against one of the huge booster rocket engines on the first stage. Tolya went first, I followed and Sergei was behind. We turned for the photographers, waved and smiled. We were there by the rocket, looking back, no time to think of what it all meant, still creatures of weird mechanisms of cosmonaut life, half of them the endless, arduous, torturous training for a seriously responsible job, the other half the temporary fame and glamour, the waving farewells and chattering cameras, the mindless inter-views and press conferences. Now the last photographs, the last smiles.

Tolya turned first, and Sergei and I quickly followed. Behind us, at the top of the steps, was an elevator cage and the man inside was waiting to take us to the top. We clambered in, huge and ungainly in our padded suits. There was hardly room for Sergei, but he pressed in and the operator swung the gate closed behind him.

Below us, the bus was already moving away. A few of the technicians stared up at us. The elevator lurched and we began to rise slowly towards the top.

I watched the body of the rocket slip by beside me. It was covered in ice! Layers and layers of ice, moulded against the metal of the rocket, condensed out of the atmosphere against the bitterly cold fuel tanks. We rose steadily through the white mist of water vapour. I glanced behind: already we seemed to have risen high into the air, but when I tipped back my head to look upwards the bulk of the rocket still stretched above us. Now we were actually close against it, rising slowly up the side of the rocket, the sheer scale of it was daunting. From the bus it had for a moment seemed surprisingly small; now it towered magnificently over me, glinting with ice in the brilliant sunshine, leaking its cold white fumes, grey and dark and tall, built for space.

When the lift arrived at the top there was a small platform giving access to the hatch. The wind was blowing stiffly up here and I could feel the platform and rocket swaying to a significant degree. We were of course insulated from the weather by our suits, but as the technicians on the platform were working in shirt-sleeves I imagine it was not unpleasant to be in.

After brief greetings all round, it was time to board the rocket. Sergei went in first; this was partly because he was in one of the two outer seats, and partly because as the engineer it was his job to make a final check of the command capsule. He would make sure that everything we had asked to be made ready was there for us, that the seats were bolted down correctly and so on. It didn't take him long and in few moments I heard him say, 'OK, you can get in now.'

It was my turn next. The staff removed the anti-scratch protective cover from my helmet and I sat down on the lip of the hatch and hauled myself in head first. One of the technicians pulled off my outer boots and then I swung my legs inside.

Beneath me was an inner hatch, leading down to the command capsule itself. I lowered myself into this feet first, turned around, then wriggled over to the right-hand seat. Sergei had already started working through his checklist.

I was now in the crew area of the rocket, and this

consisted of three main sections. At the top was the orbital capsule, an elongated sphere, which I had just passed through, and which could provide enough room for one person at a time to stretch out. This was where we would live for the two days after launch while moving to orbital rendezvous with the space station. The command capsule was slightly larger but much more cramped. The main controls for the spacecraft were located here, together with our three seats. There were two small, circular sideways-facing windows, one beside each of the outer seats. (Nothing could be seen through the windows before the launch, because the orbital and command capsules were covered by the protective fairing, which would be jettisoned as soon as we were out of the Earth's atmosphere.) Much of the room inside the command capsule was taken up by equipment that would eventually be needed during the return to Earth: parachutes, flotation gear, emergency rations, survival gear, and so on. The third module of the crew section was one to which we had no access: it contained fuel tanks, oxygen and water supplies, and the mass of ancillary equipment that ran all the on-board systems. When the Soyuz finally returned to Earth, this third stage would be used as the main retro-rocket, before being jettisoned along with the orbital capsule. Only the command capsule, the re-entry capsule, actually landed.

As soon as I was in place Tolya followed, clambering down awkwardly in the confined space and taking the third seat, in the middle. There was not an inch of free space! We were all trying to ease ourselves down into the seats, bumping elbows and reaching across each other. We had to get the smuggled stuff out of our pockets and stowed safely in the capsule, because the spacesuits were designed so exactly to the shape of our bodies that any foreign objects could cause painful pressure points during the launch. ...

Our first act on the rocket was to close the inner hatch from below, then confirm to the bunker we had done so. Not long after we heard the outer hatch being closed by one of the technicians outside on the platform. There was a muffled thud, then a clang – and it was closed.

I glanced across at the other two and sensed in them the same feeling that had suddenly swept across me. The hatch is closed. It's over. There are no more doctors, no more lectures, no more press conferences, no more smiles and salutes and last-minute tips. The hatch is closed, sealing us away from the outside world, and we are here and it's about to begin.

The three of us set to work, paging through the long checklists, each of us preoccupied by our separate tasks.

This was probably the busiest time in the whole flight: we were not only working our way down the list of checks and doing it within a set period of time, but we were also having to talk to and fro with the bunker and keep listening to what the other two crew were talking about, alert for any problems that might arise, or changes in the launch plan. In addition we had to write down various measurements in the log book: for instance, we had to keep an eye on the air pressure not only in the command capsule but in the orbital capsule too. Condensation is also a problem when there are people inside a rocket. There were several valves that had to be opened and closed at certain times and we had a little hand-pump to move the condensate from one part to another.

It required total concentration, but was worse at

some periods than at others. Some of the time there was a lot to be done in a few minutes and it was relentless: bang-bang-bang, do-it, do-it, do-it. When it was like this there was no way we could chat to each other. But then there would be short periods with nothing particular expected of us, maybe ten minutes at a time, and we would relax a bit and say a few things to each other. Even then we knew that every word we said was being relayed to the people on the ground, in the bunker, in mission control in Moscow – perhaps even to TV networks around the world. We could never be sure, so our conversation in the quiet patches tended to be about harmless physical matters. I remember, for instance, saying at one point that my feet were cold!

In fact my feet *were* cold. Thanks to a quirk of Russian spacesuit design, the ventilating air that was pumped in to keep us cool circulated best around the feet and did not seem to have much effect elsewhere. Overall I have never felt quite so hot at any other time in my life. Because of the weather, because of the physical exertions, our skin temperatures were quickly rising: a pool of warm perspiration began to collect in the small of my back, directly under me.

I was also discovering how little room I had on the right side of me, the one that was against the wall of the capsule. This was because of all the extra equipment and supplies they had shoved into the capsule that had not been there in the simulator. Tolya, against my left side, seemed to be all elbows; we were constantly bumping against each other when we moved to operate the equipment.

All through this period we were aware of continual movement and noise. The rocket was swaying perceptibly because of the wind outside and in addition we knew that all the ancillary equipment was being moved back before the launch could take place. Every now and then we would feel a shudder or vibration as something else was detached from the rocket. Each noise, each tremor through the body of the rocket, was a reminder of our isolation up there, high in the sky. In one of the quiet periods I suddenly remembered the ice crust on the main engine stage below me, the vapour rushing down towards the ground, the illusion of motion cloaking the unimaginable energy still dormant and pent up in the tanks and engines so far beneath us. That vast potential had become personal: it was there to lift *me* into space.

Immediately in front of our faces, dangling over our heads, was a little metal model of a spaceman, tied to the hatch by a piece of string. He was our talisman. All through these launch preparations the talisman swung to and fro as the rocket moved in the wind, a kind of insistent reminder of the physical world outside. It was not another good-luck charm (although it did remind me of the things people dangle inside their car windscreens), but actually had a function during the launch. Behind it was the on-board TV camera that monitored us and no matter which way the lens was turned the talisman could be seen swinging. It was a simple device for the people on the ground, who by watching its movements would be able to tell the exact moment in which we became weightless.*

Finally we got through the checklists and everything

---

*To be strictly accurate, the word 'weightless' should always be printed in inverted commas when used to describe people or things floating around inside spacecraft. Most people know in general terms what 'weightlessness' is, but it is a state which, to be accurate, is unlikely ever to be achieved.

was confirmed to be in order, as right as it would ever be. Then at last we were able to rest. Not relax. I think that is a word whose meaning is lost on any astronaut in the last few minutes before a flight – but working inside hot spacesuits, in a cramped position, is physically arduous. We were tired and it was good to rest for a while. There were still about twenty-five minutes before lift-off. The methodist came on the radio and said, 'Would you like to listen to some music? What would you like to listen to?' Music is important to the Russians, it's a relaxation. So Sergei and Tolya said they would like some and we listened to some light Russian pop: this was probably more to the taste of the people in the bunker than to Tolya himself, who I knew preferred British rock.

We were in what the Americans call the final minutes of countdown, but the system is different in Russia. There is no countdown as such. The launch is timed to the clock and we knew the exact time at which various stages would pass, but there wasn't the constant reminder of the steadily ticking clock. Instead, the controller in the bunker would come on the radio at intervals and say, 'Twenty minutes to go,' or whatever it was. We would acknowledge this, but by this time there was hardly any traffic of conversation between us.

There was at last a little time to think.

Freshest in my mind was the press conference and as soon as I thought of it I squirmed briefly inside my spacesuit at the memory. Although none of it had been my fault, I none the less blamed myself for not realising it was going to be like that and therefore for not being better prepared to deal with it. Thinking about the things I had said to my parents, I blamed myself partly for everything I had said and in equal measure for everything I had *not*. This last opportunity to speak to them frittered away in banalities! At the same time I remembered some of the things other people had said to me and these too were suddenly charged with dark significance: why had so-and-so said that and wasn't it said in an odd tone of voice? A psychologist might say that I was reacting unconsciously to the tension of these last minutes before lift-off (although if you had asked me I would have said I otherwise felt perfectly calm), but whatever the reason I felt full of belated regret and helpless to do anything about it.

In perhaps something of the same mood I started to think, for the first time ever, about similarities between me and the astronaut Christa McAuliffe, who died in the US Shuttle Challenger disaster. In recent months journalists had often asked me for my thoughts about the astronauts who had died in Challenger, presumably wondering how I felt about the prospect of being blown up. I had always shrugged off the questions, not out of bravado but because I genuinely believed the Soyuz flight was unlikely to be dangerous. And anyway, what on earth could I say, sensibly, about the prospect of being blown up in a spectacular launch explosion? However, lying there in those quiet moments before the launch began, thoughts about similarities between Christa McAuliffe and myself did go through my mind. For one thing we were both civilian women and in our different ways we had trained to be cosmonauts while surrounded by media attention. I knew many people in Britain would be watching this launch on TV, just as the Challenger launch had caught the attention of millions of ordinary Americans, and in particular we were both the focus of much interest from school-children. She, like me, had sat there high inside a space vehicle, waiting for the torch to be lit beneath her. I thought, 'It couldn't happen twice, could it?' In that thought, of course, similarity died. Logic took over: she had had no precedent on which to dwell while the seconds ticked away and in any event the chances of my suffering an accidental death were neither raised nor lowered by hers. I wished I could have met and known her before she died, because we would probably have had a lot in common, but it would be pretentious and untrue to say I felt spiritually close to her.

I felt closer, spiritually and practically, with other people who had flown on Soyuz missions. For instance, one of the cosmonauts on the mission before mine had been a journalist from Japan called Toyohiro Akiyama. This was a purely commercial flight: the television station Toyohiro worked for had paid all the expenses in order to buy themselves an exclusive story. I had met Toyohiro in Star City and he told me that before starting the training he was completely unfit: he was a two-packs-a-day smoker and the heaviest thing he had ever lifted was a pen. He had gone through the training, though, those long months of physical and mental discipline, and at the end of it he emerged as a fully capable cosmonaut, fit as a fiddle, part of a profes- sional team. Toyohiro had worked for and earned his place.

I had been down to Baikonur the previous December to watch Toyohiro's launch and it had made a profound impression on me. As I lay in my command capsule, waiting for the moment of launch to arrive, I felt I knew and understood a large part of what the people outside would be experiencing. The wait for ignition seemed interminable out there, because there was little hint of the activity inside the rocket and in the bunker. When the launch finally began the sheer spectacle of the rocket rising into the sky and the shattering noise that went with it were unforgettable. Then the long minutes craning my neck, watching the ever-diminishing flare of brilliant white light, the quickly vanishing exhaust trail. When even this last trace could no longer be seen everyone crammed around the TV monitors, because they were the only things left for us to look at. At the end, when the rocket was so far away even the TV link was lost, I gazed across the scrubland at the launch site once more. The platform was less than a mile away, empty now and silent, and I found that spectacle inexpressibly moving. I had turned away, feeling drained.

In my earphones, a voice from the bunker said, 'Five minutes to go. Please close the masks of your helmets.'

The three of us obeyed, then confirmed. Our call-sign was OZONE, and we identified ourselves by crew number. I was the last to confirm, and so I said, 'OZONE 3, OZONE 3, my helmet is shut. We are in the preparation régime, ready to go.'

The bunker replied, 'Understood, OZONE 3. We are also in that régime. Everything on board is correct and we are now ready to launch.'

A little later, the voice said, 'Two minutes.'

Then it said, 'One minute.'

Now that we were not moving around or reaching for the controls above us, it was comfortable to be sitting there in the spacesuit. I glanced at the little talisman, swinging from the hatch above us. I felt the pressure of Tolya's elbow against mine. I could hear the quiet hiss of static in the speaker against my ear. Sergei said nothing, Tolya said nothing; the voice from the bunker was silent. It was a moment of stillness, of final waiting. My feet were still cold.

Far away, deep below, there came a rumbling noise as the rocket engines ignited. On the control panel the on-board clock had started automatically; we were nominally one second into the mission, then two, and the engines still rumbled far below. Three seconds, and the rumbling grew louder, and the four launch-gantries swung away. I could feel vibration but no sense of acceleration. I knew we must have left the ground and were in that momentary limbo where the rocket seems to balance precariously on its thrust, surely destined to topple. But the engines continued to roar beneath us and the instruments confirmed that we were away from the tower, that acceleration was beginning to build, and we could feel the pressure of g-forces growing steadily against us.

When I next looked at the clock we were twenty seconds into the flight and above us the talisman was taut on its string, no longer as free to swing. I could now sense the rocket's power not only from the vibrations coming through the seat but also from the increasing press of acceleration. The clock showed that forty seconds had elapsed. The voice from the bunker confirmed the successful launch and Sergei briefly responded. G-forces continued to grow; the rocket was getting lighter as the fuel burned away and we were picking up speed.

After 115 seconds came the first of several loud bumps and bangs: the escape rocket on the nose of the craft was being jettisoned. At this point we were 46 kilometres from the ground, on the threshold of space. Three seconds later there was another jolt, this one bigger and from below, as the first-stage booster rockets separated from us. This was the moment we passed the 50 kilometres mark, the height the Russians usually designate as the beginning of space.

Our smooth acceleration continued as the rocket grew lighter; now we were using the second-stage engine. This was the centrally mounted main engine, used from the moment of lift-off. It was still burning steadily when, 165 seconds into the flight, the protective fairing that covered the windows was jettisoned, no longer needed to protect the spacecraft from the atmosphere as there was little atmosphere left outside!

Sunlight streamed in. I looked down at the Earth. We were already over the Pacific!

Tolya said, 'What can you see? What can you see?' He had no window, and was dazzled by the golden sunlight pouring in.

I could see the curvature of the Earth! Speckly white clouds! A brilliant azure sea! The blackness of space! Now I knew I was where the theory told me I should be – out from the world, above the blue skies and diamond-studded clouds. Dreams sometimes do come true and I felt so alive!

The craft was rotating and the view turned away from me. Then it was Sergei's turn to see. Poor Tolya could only glimpse it.

Sergei said, 'It's snowing up here! The ice is breaking off!'

In the sunlight, in the vacuum outside my window, I too could see that chunks of ice were breaking away from the body of the rocket. If we had been in the atmosphere they would have been whipped out of our sight before we saw them, but here they spun away from the craft and we only left them behind because we were still accelerating.

The second stage separated after 288 seconds: another jolt, another bang sensed through the metal of the rocket, and for a brief moment our bodies felt lighter, almost as if they were about to drift out of our seats. I saw the talisman above me tremble, seeming to dither between floating and swinging, but then the third stage fired and tremendous acceleration immediately pressed us down again. The rocket had much less mass now and this final engine set about the last part of our launch in a fierce and energetic way. G-forces rose to a respectable $3\frac{1}{2}$ g. The flight was at last thrilling me with the sensation of speed.

I glanced at the on-board clock. Five hundred seconds had elapsed since we lifted away from the pad. Just eight minutes ago I had been bound to the Earth's surface, now I was in space. Eight minutes ago my family had been less than a mile away from me; now we were not even on the same planet.

At 530 seconds the third stage cut out and was jettisoned. It did not happen gradually. One moment it was burning ferociously behind me, in the next it stopped completely. One moment I was being pressed hard into my seat and in the next I was not. I had been straining against the g-force without realizing I had been doing so; then I stopped straining. Quite involuntarily, I said, '*Uhh!*'

Beside me, Sergei and Tolya said, '*Uhh!*'

The talisman was no longer tense against its string. It hovered by the hatch, the string snaking loosely towards it. It had suddenly become, as we had suddenly become, weightless.

A Glimpse of the Future?

from *Subterranean Gothic*

by Paul Theroux

Paul Theroux travels on the New York subway... 'a serious matter – the rackety train, the silent passengers, the occasional scream...'.

When people say the subway frightens them, they are not being silly or irrational. It is no good saying how cheap or how fast it is. The subway *is* frightening. It is also very easy to get lost in the subway, and the person who is lost in New York City has a serious problem. New Yorkers make it their business to avoid getting lost.

It is the stranger who gets lost. It is the stranger who follows people hurrying into the stair-well: subway entrances are just dark holes in the sidewalk – the stations are below ground. There is nearly always a bus-stop near the subway entrance. People waiting at a bus-stop have a special pitying gaze for people entering the subway. It is sometimes not pity, but fear, bewilderment, curiosity, or fatalism; often they look like miners' wives watching their menfolk going down the pit.

The stranger's sense of disorientation down below is immediate. The station is all tile and iron and dampness; it has bars and turnstiles and steel grates. It has the look of an old prison or a monkey cage.

Buying a token, the stranger may ask directions, but the token booth – reinforced, burglar-proof, bullet-proof – renders the reply incoherent. And subway directions are a special language: 'A train...

Downtown ... Express to the Shuttle ... Change at Ninety-sixth for the two ... Uptown ... The Lex ... CC ... LL ... The Local ... '

Most New Yorkers refer to the subway by the now-obsolete forms 'IND', 'IRT', 'BMT'. No one intentionally tries to confuse the stranger; it is just that, where the subway is concerned, precise directions are very hard to convey.

Verbal directions are incomprehensible, written ones are defaced. The signboards and subway maps are indiscernible beneath layers of graffiti. ...

Graffiti is destructive; it is anti-art; it is an act of violence, and it can be deeply menacing. It has displaced the subway signs and maps, blacked-out the windows of the trains and obliterated the instructions. *In case of emergency* – is cross-hatched with a felt-tip. *These seats are for the elderly and disabled* – a yard-long signature obscures it. *The subway tracks are very dangerous; if the train should stop, do not* – the rest is black and unreadable. The stranger cannot rely on printed instructions or warnings, and there are few cars out of the six thousand on the system in which the maps have not been torn out. Assuming the stranger has boarded the train, he or she can feel only panic when, searching for a clue to his route, he sees in the map-frame the message, *Guzmán – Ladrón, Maricón y Asesino.*

Panic: and so he gets off the train, and then his troubles really begin.

He may be in the South Bronx or the upper reaches of Broadway on the Number 1 line, or on any one of a dozen lines that traverse Brooklyn. He gets off the train, which is covered in graffiti, and steps on to a station platform which is covered in graffiti. It is possible (this is true of many stations) that none of the signs will be legible. Not only will the stranger not know where he is, but the stairways will be splotched and stinking – no *Uptown*, no *Downtown*, no *Exit*. It is also possible that not a single soul will be around, and the most dangerous stations – ask any police officer – are the emptiest. . . .

This is the story that most people tell of subways fear. In every detail it is like a nightmare, complete with rats and mice and a tunnel and a low ceiling. It is manifest suffocation, straight out of Poe.[1] Those who tell this story seldom have a crime to report. They have experienced fear. It is completely understandable – what is worse than being trapped underground? – but it has been a private horror. In most cases, the person will have come to no harm. He will, however, remember his fear on that empty station for the rest of his life.

When New Yorkers recount an experience like this they are invariably speaking of something that happened on another line, not their usual route. Their own line is fairly safe, they'll say; it's cleaner than the others; it's got a little charm, it's kind of dependable; they've been taking it for years. Your line has crazy people on it, but my line has 'characters'. This sense of loyalty to a regularly used line is the most remarkable thing about the subway passenger in New York. It is, in fact, a jungle attitude.

In any jungle, the pathway is a priority. People move around New York in various ways, but the complexities of the subway have allowed the New Yorker to think of his own route as something personal, even *original*. No one uses maps on the subway – you seldom see any.

---

[1] Edgar Allan Poe (1809–49). One of America's greatest writers, especially famous for his tales of terror.

Most subway passengers were shown how to ride it by parents or friends. Then habit turns it into instinct, just like a trot down a jungle path. The passenger knows where he is going because he never diverges from his usual route. But that is also why, unless you are getting off at precisely his stop, he cannot tell you how to get where you're going.

In general, people have a sense of pride in their personal route; they may be superstitious about it and even a bit secretive. Vaguely fearful of other routes, they may fantasise about them – these 'dangerous' lines that run through unknown districts. This provokes them to assign a specific character to the other lines. The IRT is the oldest line; for some people it is dependable, with patches of elegance (those beaver mosaics at Astor Place), and for others it is dangerous and dirty. One person praises the IND, another person damns it. 'I've got a soft spot for the BMT,' a woman told me, but found it hard to explain why. 'Take the A train,' I was told. 'That's the best one, like the song.' But some of the worst stations are on the (very long) A line. The CC, 8th Avenue local, was described to me as 'scuzz' – disreputable – but this train, running from Bedford Park Boulevard, the Bronx, via Manhattan and Brooklyn, to Rockaway Park, Queens, covers a distance of some thirty-two miles. The fact is that for some of these miles it is pleasant and for others it is not. There is part of one line that is indisputably bad; that is the stretch of the 2 line (IRT) from Nostrand to New Lots Avenue. It is dangerous and ugly and when you get to New Lots Avenue you cannot imagine why you went. The police call this line 'The Beast'.

But people in the know – the police, the Transit Authority, the people who travel throughout the system – say that one line is pretty much like another.

No line is entirely good or bad, crime-ridden or crime-free. The trains carry crime with them, picking it up in one area and bringing it to another. They pass through a district and take on the characteristics of that place. The South Bronx is regarded as a high-risk area, but seven lines pass through it, taking vandals and thieves all over the system. There is a species of vandalism that was once peculiar to the South Bronx: boys would swing on the stanchions – those chrome poles in the centre of the car – and, raising themselves sideways until they were parallel with the floor, they would kick hard against a window and break it. Now this South Bronx window-breaking technique operates throughout the system. This business about one line being dependable and another being charming and a third being dangerous is just jungle talk.

The most-mugged man in New York must be the white-haired creaky-looking fellow in Bedford-Stuyvesant who has had as many as thirty mugging attempts made on him in a single year. And he still rides the subway trains. He's not as crazy as he looks: he's a cop in the Transit Police, a plain-clothes man who works with the Mobile Task Force in the district designated 'Brooklyn North'. This man is frequently a decoy. In the weeks before Christmas he rode the J and the GG and the 2 lines looking like a pathetic senior citizen, with two gaily-wrapped parcels in his shopping bag. He was repeatedly ambushed by unsuspecting muggers, and then he pulled out his badge and handcuffs and arrested his attackers.

Muggers are not always compliant. Then the Transit Police Officer unholsters his pistol, but not before jamming a coloured headband over his head to alert any nearby uniformed officer. Before the advent of headbands many plain-clothes men were shot by their colleagues in uniform.

'And then we rush in,' says Sergeant Donnery of the Mobile Task Force. 'Ninety per cent of the guys out there can kick my ass, one on one. You've got to come on yelling and screaming. "You so-and-so! You so-and-so! I'm going to kill you!" Unless the suspect is deranged and has a knife or something. In that case you might have to talk quietly. But if the guy's tough and you go in meek you get sized up very fast.'

The Transit Police has three thousand officers and thirteen dogs. It is one of the biggest police forces in the United States and is altogether independent from the New York City Police, though the pay and training are exactly the same. It is so independent the men cannot speak to each other on their radios, which many Transit Police find inconvenient when chasing a suspect up the subway stairs into the street.

What about the dogs? 'Dogs command respect,' I was told at Transit Police Headquarters. 'Think of them as a tool, like a gun or a nightstick. At the moment it's just a test programme for high-crime stations, late-night hours, that kind of thing.'

I wondered aloud whether it would work, and the reply was, 'A crime is unlikely to be committed anywhere near one of these dogs.'

The Canine Squad is housed with a branch of the Mobile Task Force at the underground junction of the LL and GG lines: Lorimer Street–Metropolitan Avenue. The bulletin board on the plain-clothes men's side is plastered with unit citations and merit awards, and Sgt Donnery of the Task Force was recently made 'Cop of the Month' for a particularly clever set of arrests. Sgt Donnery is in charge of thirty-two plain-clothes men and two detectives. Their motto is

'Soar with the Eagles'. A sheaf of admiring news-paper clippings testifies to their effectiveness. As we talked, the second shift was preparing to set out for the day.

'Morale seems very high,' I said. The men were joking, watching the old-man decoy spraying his hair and beard white.

'Sure, morale is high,' Sgt Donnery said. 'We feel we're getting something accomplished. It isn't easy. Sometimes you have to hide in a porter's room with a mop for four days before you get your man. We dress up as porters, conductors, motormen, track-workers. If there are a lot of robberies and track-workers in the same station, we dress up as track-workers. We've got all the uniforms.'

'Plain-clothes men' is something of a misnomer for the Task Force that has enough of a theatrical wardrobe to mount a production of *Subways are for Sleeping*.

And yet, looking at Howard Haag and Joseph Minucci standing on the platform at Nassau Avenue on the GG line, you would probably take them for a pair of physical-education teachers on the way to the school gym. They look tough, but not aggressively so; they are healthy and well-built – but some of that is padding: they both wear bullet-proof vests. Underneath the ordinary clothes the men are well armed. Each man carries a .38, a blackjack and a can of Mace. Minucci has a two-way radio.

Haag has been on the force for seventeen years, Minucci for almost seven. Neither has in that time ever fired his gun, though each has an excellent arrest-record and a pride in detection. They are funny, alert and indefatigable, and together they make Starsky and Hutch look like a pair of hysterical cream-puffs. Their job is also much harder than any City cop's. I had been told repeatedly that the average City cop would refuse to work in the conditions that the Transit Police endure every day. At Nassau Avenue, Minucci told me why.

'Look at the stations! They're dirty, they're cold, they're noisy. If you fire your gun you'll kill about ten innocent people – you're trapped here. You stand here some days and the cold and the dampness creep into your bones and you start shivering. And that smell – smell it? – it's like that all the time, and you've got to stand there and breathe it in. Bergen Street Station, the snow comes through the bars and you freeze. They call it "The Ice-Box". Then some days, kids recognise you – they've seen you make a collar – and they swear at you, call you names, try to get you to react, smoke pot right under your nose. "Here come the DT's" – that's what they call us. It's the conditions. They're awful. You have to take so much crap from these schoolkids. And your feet are killing you. So you sit down, read a newspaper, drink coffee, and then you get a rip from a shoofly –'

Minucci wasn't angry; he said all this in a smiling, ironical way. Like Howie Haag, he enjoys his work and takes it seriously. A 'shoofly', he explained, is a police-inspector who rides the subway looking for officers who are goldbricking – though having a coffee on a cold day hardly seemed to me like goldbricking. 'We're not supposed to drink coffee,' Minucci said, and he went on to define other words in the Transit Police vocabulary: 'lushworker' (a person who robs drunks or sleeping passengers); and 'Flop Squad' (decoys who pretend to be asleep, in order to attract lushworkers).

Just then, as we were talking at Nassau, the station filled up with shouting boys – big ones, aged anywhere from fifteen to eighteen. There were hundreds of them and, with them, came the unmistakable odour of smouldering marijuana. They were boys from Automotive High School, heading south on the GG. They stood on the platform howling and screaming and sucking smoke out of their fingers, and when the train pulled in they began fighting towards the doors.

'You might see one of these kids being a pain in the neck, writing graffiti or smoking dope or something,' Howie Haag said. 'And you might wonder why we don't do anything. The reason is we're looking for something serious – robbers, snatchers, assault, stuff like that.'

Minucci said, 'The Vandalism Squad deals with window-kickers and graffiti. Normally we don't.'

Once on the train the crowd of yelling boys thinned out. I had seen this sort of activity before: boys get on the subway train and immediately bang through the connecting doors and walk from car to car. I asked Minucci why this was so.

'They're marking the people. See them? They're looking for an old lady near a door or something they can snatch, or a pocket they can pick. They're sizing up the situation. They're also heading for the last car. That's where they hang out on this train.'

Howie said, 'They want to see if we'll follow them. If we do, they'll mark us as cops.'

Minucci and Haag did not follow, though at each stop they took cautious looks out of the train, using the reflections in mirrors and windows.

'They play the doors when it's crowded,' Minucci said.

Howie said, 'School-kids can take over a train.'

'Look at that old lady,' Minucci said. 'She's doing everything wrong.'

The woman, in her late sixties, was sitting next to the door. Her wristwatch was exposed and her handbag dangled from the arm closest to the door. Minucci

23

explained that one of the commonest subway crimes was inspired by this posture. The snatcher reached through the door from the platform and, just before the doors shut, he grabbed the bag or watch, or both; and then he was off, and the train was pulling out, with the victim trapped on board.

I wondered whether the plain-clothes men would warn her. They didn't. But they watched her closely, and when she got off they escorted her in an anonymous way. The old woman never knew how well protected she was and how any person making a move to rob her would have been hammered flat to the platform by the combined weight of Officers Minucci and Haag.

There were men on the train drinking wine out of bottles sheathed in paper bags. Such men are everywhere in New York, propped against walls, with bottle and bag. A few hours earlier, at Myrtle-Willoughby, I had counted forty-six men hanging around outside a housing project, drinking this way. I had found their idleness and their stares and their drunken slouching a little sinister.

Minucci said, 'The winos don't cause much trouble. It's the kids coming home from school. They're the majority of snatchers and robbers.'

Minucci went on, 'On the LL line, on Grant Street, there's much more crime than before, because Eastern District High School relocated there. It's mostly larceny and bag snatches.'

It was a salutary experience for me, riding through Brooklyn with Officers Minucci and Haag. Who, except a man flanked by two armed plain-clothes men, would travel from one end of Brooklyn to the other, walking through housing projects and derelict areas, and waiting for hours at subway stations? It was a perverse hope of mine that we would happen upon a crime, or even be the victims of a mugging-attempt. We were left alone, things were quiet, there were no arrests; but for the first time in my life I was travelling the hinterland of New York City with my head up, looking people in the eye with curiosity and lingering scrutiny and no fear. It is a shocking experience. I felt at first, because of my bodyguards, like Haile Selassie;[2] and then I seemed to be looking at an alien land – I had never had the courage to gaze at it so steadily. It was a land impossible to glamorise and hard to describe. I had the feeling I was looking at the future.

[2] Emperor of Ethiopia (1930–74)

A Decision

from *Tracing it Home:*
Journeys around a Chinese Family

by Lynn Pan

Lynn Pan's family, like millions of others, were exiled from their
home in China by the Communists in 1949. Everything had
been left behind. In 1978, on the first anniversary of her
mother's death in London, her family have arranged for
ceremonies to be performed for her mother's soul in Hong
Kong. Ah Sam, the maid of Lynn Pan's aunt, has organised it
all.

The last event of the day was the burning of paper
'spirit' money and objects for my mother's use in the
next world. Times had changed since burying a person
properly meant filling the tomb with mortuary goods,
pottery models of possessions such as its occupant
could do with in heaven. Nowadays, to keep the dead in
the style to which they had become accustomed in life,
one commissions paper mock-ups of objects of earthly
desire (such as a house complete with a three-piece
suite, doll's-house furnishings and even servants). I was
sorry times had changed, thinking of those wonderful
ceramics archaeologists had unearthed from ancient
Chinese tombs.

It was late afternoon when, following Ah Sam, I
strolled down the path leading from the temple court-
yard to where the burning was to take place. It was a
cleft in the hill on which the temple stood. The treasure
heap, looking highly combustible and somehow lonely,
became a pyre; from a cloud of humid smoke, through

which near and distant objects appeared to billow, ash fell plentifully. The others stayed only a few minutes, and Ah Sam and I were the only two to remain.

We were standing there, not speaking, when Ah Sam suddenly turned to me and said, 'A car.' Her voice sounded regretful, as though she were responsible.

'We forgot to include a motor car,' she went on; 'your mother drove one, didn't she?' With her Toyota missing, how was she to get about in the other world?

I looked back from Ah Sam to the conflagration, hiding my smile. I felt an epoch instead of a mere generation separated me from Ah Sam, and I also suspected that I was the poorer for being further cut off from folk and faith.

This talk of cars made me think of my mother first learning to drive. It was in Malaya, and the car she drove was a second-hand jeep. It seemed altogether wrong. The thing was, my mother was an elegant woman, a person of pampered indoor breeding; that was the great and touching thing about her driving us children so determinedly from house to school, school to house, under the scorching sun, sweat and dust mingling on her fine, fair skin.

But at the time my father could afford nothing better; it was as simple as that. He was a newly arrived immigrant in a strange tropical country, stripped of everything he had once owned and struggling to make a fresh start. To go from a Lagonda classic sports car in swanky Old Shanghai to a rusty jeep in the jungles of Malaya was indeed a comedown, but for people of my parents' class, that was revolution in a nutshell.

Our house had no electricity or running water. Mosquitoes stung us on face and arms; sores from infected bites scarred our legs. In the house ants crawled around cups or carried dead upturned cockroaches or beetles away like pallbearers. Lizards darted after insects on walls, their tails sometimes dropping on to the table and into the cups. My mother taught her children to read and told them stories by the light of a kerosene lamp. She looked elegant still, but the hands that held the book were roughened. A daughter died, then a son, and all because the hospitals were inadequate.

Hard as Malaya was, there was no question of going back to China, or even of going to Hong Kong, *the* place for refugee capitalists from Shanghai, their second eldorado. After leaving Shanghai, my father had started a business as a stock and exchange broker in Hong Kong, but although this enterprise had flourished for a while, the skies had suddenly collapsed upon him. It is hard to determine what exactly happened; I think his partner, one of the many adopted sons of Silas Hardoon, the well-known Jewish tycoon in Shanghai, was at least partly to blame. At any rate my father lost a fortune, and bankruptcy was all that was left.

With no money to speak of, and a family to support, my father's position was desperate. He was prepared to try almost anything – even the backwoods of Malaya, about which he knew nothing beyond the rumour that there might be opportunities there. Malaya was 'South Seas' to him: going there must have seemed as final as a step into the unknown, a hazardous passage to another life, from which no one returned the same.

And so it proved. Going to Malaya, he buried at last his dream of returning one day to Shanghai. I once heard him say to a friend, 'For ten years I thought I would go back; for ten years I looked back, not forward.' In an old Chinese story you would wake after ten years to find it had all been a dream. Only this was history, and he counted himself lucky that he awoke to it before it was too late. His looking forward affected us children. In England, where I came to study, I would be asked, 'Ever been to China?' And I would answer, 'Long ago.' China had become the long ago, the memory.

My mother's strength carried her through her uprooting. She did what she must. With that emphatic quality of hers, she grasped the nettle – though the nettle grasped remained no less a nettle. Her inability to find in her displacement and successful adjustment any cause for self-pity or congratulation was the Chinese in her; it is only the English, enjoying stability in their country for so long, who use words like 'courage' and 'dignity' of people who rise above the smallest dislocation. My mother did not cling to her memories of a lost land; her reminiscences of Shanghai were not a case of trying to call back her yesterday. Though I was made aware at an early age of how glorious life had been in Shanghai (was it Talleyrand who said, 'He who has not lived before the revolution shall never know the sweetness of life'?), that awareness was merged with a sense of severance, such as one gets from contemplating the world before a war.

What struck me now, standing by the ashes of my mother's 'spirit' possessions, was the completeness of that severance. The measure of it was the fact that she had been dead a year, and her own mother, living in China, had no inkling of it; indeed might never get to hear of it, if the wish was to spare her. In that respect the Bamboo Curtain was not a source of difficulty, but ease.

Simultaneously there came to my mind all those ads you saw in Chinese newspapers in Hong Kong of fathers looking for their sons, mothers for their daughters, sisters for their brothers. ('WANG SHUCHUN SEEKS SON TIAN JINFENG: Tian Jinfeng, aged fifty-nine,

29

formerly of Dacheng County, Hebei Province, left with the Kuomintang Army in 1949 for Taiwan, and has not been heard of since. His mother, now seventy-nine, desires a reunion in the time left to her. Anyone who has news of him please write to Wang Shuchun, Songji Hamlet, Dacheng County, Hebei Province.') I have always wondered what the success rate of these Wanted columns was: did Wang Shuchun become reunited with her son? What if he was already dead? How would it be for her to learn from some stranger answering the ad that all this time her son's death had lain in wait for her discovery, an unknown and terrible loss in store?

The Chinese have learned the acceptance of separation as an unremarkable norm of life. Yet all of a sudden it seemed incredible to me that you could die without your mother hearing of it. I was thinking of my mother, then of myself; I was thinking, I could have died before you, there are only nineteen years between us. One is apt to think of one's parents as old; yet my mother was young to have died – too young yet to set store by her memories. Was that why she gave the impression of having done for good with that part of her life that was lived in China, as though who one is *isn't* where one comes from?

With this thought there came a dense tangle of many others, until the voice of Ah Sam broke in with, 'Shall we go back?'

I think it was at that moment that the idea of going back to China began to form itself and to stand waiting in a corner of my mind.

The Summit

from *A Description of the Scenery of*
the Lakes in the North of England

by William Wordsworth

This extract from a guidebook to Cumberland, first published
in 1810, became so popular that one clergyman asked
eagerly if the author had ever written anything else. Of course,
this particular travel writer was the great poet William
Wordsworth. Wordsworth's description went through five
editions in his lifetime, proving his prose to be as haunting as
his poems.

Having left Rosthwaite in Borrowdale on a bright
morning in the first week of October, we ascended from
Seathwaite to the top of the ridge, called Ash-course,
and thence beheld three distinct views; – on one side,
the continuous Vale of Borrowdale, Keswick, and
Bassenthwaite, – with Skiddaw, Helvellyn, Saddle-back,
and numerous other mountains, – and, in the distance,
the Solway Frith and the Mountains of Scotland; – on
the other side, and below us, the Langdale Pikes – their
own vale below *them*; – Windermere, – and, far beyond
Windermere, Ingleborough in Yorkshire. But how shall
I speak of the deliciousness of the third prospect! At
this time, *that* was most favoured by sunshine and
shade. The green Vale of Esk – deep and green, with its
glittering serpent stream, lay below us; and on we
looked to the mountains near the sea, – Black Comb
pre-eminent, – and, still beyond, to the sea itself, in
dazzling brightness. Turning round we saw the
mountains of Wastdale in tumult; to our right, Great

31

Gavel, the loftiest, a distinct and *huge* form, though the middle of the mountain was, to our eyes, as its base.

We had attained the object of this journey; but our ambition now mounted higher. We saw the summit of Scawfell, apparently very near to us; and we shaped our course towards it; but, discovering that it could not be reached without first making a considerable descent, we resolved instead to aim at another point of the same mountain, called the *Pikes*, which I have since found has been estimated as higher than the summit bearing the name of Scawfell Head, where the Stone Man is built.

The sun had never once been overshadowed by a cloud during the whole of our progress from the centre of Borrowdale. On the summit of the Pike, which we gained after much toil, though without difficulty, there was not a breath of air to stir even the papers containing our refreshment, as they lay spread out upon a rock. The stillness seemed to be not of this world: – we paused, and kept silence to listen; and no sound could be heard: the Scawfell Cataracts were voiceless to us; and there was not an insect to hum in the air. The vales which we had seen from Ash-course lay yet in view; and side by side with Eskdale we now saw the sister Vale of Donnerdale terminated by the Duddon Sands. But the majesty of the mountains below, and close to us, is not to be conceived. We now beheld the whole mass of Great Gavel from its base, – the Den of Wastdale at our feet – a gulf immeasurable; Grasmere and the other mountains of Crummock; Ennerdale and its mountains; and the sea beyond! We sat down to our repast, and gladly would we have tempered our beverage (for there was no spring or well near us) with such a supply of delicious water as we might have procured had we been on the rival summit of Great Gavel; for on its highest point is a small triangular receptacle in the native rock, which, the shepherds say, is never dry. There we might have slaked our thirst plenteously with a pure and celestial liquid, for the cup or basin, it appears, has no other feeder than the dews of heaven, the showers, the vapours, the hoar frost, and the spotless snow.

While we were gazing around, 'Look,' I exclaimed, 'at yon ship upon the glittering sea!' 'Is it a ship?' replied our shepherd-guide. 'It can be nothing else,' interposed my companion; 'I cannot be mistaken, I am so accustomed to the appearance of ships at sea.' The guide dropped the argument; but before a minute was gone he quietly said, 'Now look at your ship; it is changed into a horse.' So indeed it was, – a horse with a gallant neck and head. We laughed heartily; and, I hope, when again inclined to be positive, I may remember the ship and the horse upon the glittering sea; and the calm confidence, yet submissiveness, of our wise Man of the Mountains, who certainly had more knowledge of clouds than we, whatever might be our knowledge of ships.

I know not how long we might have remained on the summit of the Pike, without a thought of moving, had not our guide warned us that we must not linger; for a storm was coming. We looked in vain to espy the signs of it. Mountains, vales, and sea were touched with the clear light of the sun. 'It is there,' said he, pointing to the sea beyond Whitehaven, and there we perceived a light vapour unnoticeable but by a shepherd accustomed to watch all mountain bodings. We gazed around again, and yet again, unwilling to lose the remembrance of what lay before us in that lofty solitude; and then prepared to depart. Meanwhile the air changed to cold, and we saw that tiny vapour swelled into mighty masses of cloud which came boiling over

33

the mountains. Great Gavel, Helvellyn, and Skiddaw, were wrapped in storm; yet Langdale, and the mountains in that quarter, remained all bright in sunshine. Soon the storm reached us; we sheltered under a crag; and almost as rapidly as it had come it passed away, and left us free to observe the struggles of gloom and sunshine in other quarters. Langdale now had its share, and the Pikes of Langdale were decorated by two splendid rainbows. Skiddaw also had his own rainbows. Before we again reached Ash-course every cloud had vanished from every summit.

I ought to have mentioned that round the top of Scawfell-Pike not a blade of grass is to be seen. Cushions or tufts of moss, parched and brown, appear between the huge blocks and stones that lie in heaps on all sides to a great distance, like skeletons or bones of the earth not needed at the creation, and there left to be covered with never-dying lichens, which the clouds and dews nourish; and adorn with colours of vivid and exquisite beauty. Flowers, the most brilliant feathers, and even gems, scarcely surpass in colouring some of those masses of stone, which no human eye beholds, except the shepherd or traveller be led thither by curiosity: and how seldom must this happen! For the other eminence is the one visited by the adventurous stranger; and the shepherd has no inducement to ascend the Pike in quest of his sheep; no food being *there* to tempt them.

We certainly were singularly favoured in the weather; for when we were seated on the summit, our conductor, turning his eyes thoughtfully round, said, 'I do not know that in my whole life I was ever, at any season of the year, so high upon the mountains on so *calm* a day.' (It was the seventh of October.) Afterwards we had a spectacle of the grandeur of earth and heaven commingled; yet without terror. We knew that the storm would pass away, for so our prophetic guide had assured us.

Before we reached Seathwaite in Borrowdale, a few stars had appeared, and we pursued our way down the Vale, to Rosthwaite, by moonlight.

Parents

from *Traveller's Prelude*

by Freya Stark

Dame Freya Stark, famous for her own travels, recounts here
the journey that her mother made to join her father: a journey
that not only brought her to the particular place that he loved,
but to a wholly different and very challenging way of life.

If we could make contours in hearts as we do in maps,
to see their loves, we should learn what strange unexpected regions attain the deepest depth. Often we
might discover that a place rather than a person holds
the secret. It was so with my father. The wild country of
Dartmoor, where he had walked as a small boy, was to
him a dark and refreshing well, from which the water of
his life was drawn. It gave him silent serenity, and a sort
of patient endurance, very like its own high and gentle,
cloud-receiving hills. It was a very remote country in his
boyhood, a long day's drive with pony carriage or ride
on horseback from Torquay; and even when he
brought my mother there as a seventeen-year-old bride,
and in my own childhood twenty years later, the train
from Newton Abbot was a shabby little country train
waiting in a neglected siding like a pony with a coat
worn bare in patches, for the G.W.R. gave it only old
coaches whose velvet showed edges of wear. Metal foot-
warmers were laid down the middle of every compartment on the floor, and my mother remembered an old
farmer getting in and squatting down on one of them
on a winter's day, remarking: 'It's sartainly kind of the

Company to think for'm comfort.'

When the train reached Moretonhampstead, a pony carriage was waiting in the station yard; another footwarmer; feet packed in straw; the rug tucked about one. The seven miles drew out unending among hills with fields of turnips, grass or clover, or ribbed loam, and in winter the shadows of hedges wheeling across the snow. There was no asphalt, then, but the road dried quickly, its puddles lined with pebbles whose glistening granite edges never lose their sharpness; they shone with a clearness that I always associate with Dartmoor after rain. Ruts dipped in and out of them like ribbons, with a ruffle of curled mud at the edge: and when we had climbed to where Chagford spills itself on its hills, and had driven by whitewashed cottages under thatched roofs where only a notice in a window showed a shop inside; and had trotted down with the brake squeaking and the pony's neck well back and wrinkled under the tautened reins – then we began to ascend longer slopes and to dip less deeply, ever gaining on the brown fortress whose horizontal rocks lay wrapped in Atlantic mists or sleeping in the sun. Half-way up the last slope, where fields and cultivation end, rough walls of granite take the place of hedges, and a swing-gate eaten with lichen spans the roads to keep the cattle on their open moor. Here, even when it rains, the tilt of land is too sharp for mud, and runnels of clear water trickle through the turf. Trees lean away from the south-west wind, until only thorn and the mountain ash continue to hold fast where walls or boulders give shelter for their roots. The roads lead to some last lonely farm, or peter out into a deep-rutted soft track on the way towards it, while a great freedom of solitary breastlike ridges opens on every side. Here the farms and villages that had 'moor rights' could put their ponies and flocks and the small tough cattle with blunt muzzles and flat foreheads, that flourish on moor weather, to wander at will. In the height of summer a rare cart would jolt across collecting the farmer's sods of peat, cut and stacked in small rows, two by two like tents, to dry in the precarious sun. A lark would hang over the silence, remembered as one remembers an aeroplane today, a filler of spaces; a lapwing fluttered from the wind-singing heather with pretended lameness to draw away the passing stranger from her nest; and rabbits made holes in dykes of short-bladed grass, boundaries of the moor.

My father knew this country and from boyhood went about it. He was a good rider and fond of breaking in his own horses; but he preferred to walk so as to watch the life about him more closely, and he knew plants and animals, and could find his way at night by the set of a star on a ridge where most people saw only the uniform pathless darkness of the moors.

He was well-knit, neither short nor tall, with a body whose muscles all were used and a face in which the grey eyes were remembered because they were so honest. He liked knee-breeches for walking. He had the slim beautiful ankles that many Englishmen have who live in the country, and wore easy shoes, and thick woollen stockings that Kate Kegan knitted in Torquay. Stepping behind him as we learned to do in our childhood across the boggy places, we saw his feet as easy on the moors as the heather they trod on, whose wiry tendons spring back and recover when they are pressed in passing; or as the pony that grazes at will and leaves the slant of its hoof in the peat to tell the direction in which it went. My father seemed always to make a harmony with these weather-beaten things. In his tweeds, shapeless and soaked with showers, he was at home; and my earliest English memories show him putting on an old Burberry to go for a walk for pleasure in the rain.

In the early time, before I was born, he had no house near Dartmoor, but used to stay at one or other of the farms where rooms were let to summer visitors. Their fenced gardens are crammed with flowers, and sedums blossom and mosses grow along the edges of their thatch. But it is safer to put all sheets out to dry before going to bed, for the whitewashed walls are usually wet if you press a hand against them; and though in the sitting-room some warmth can be coaxed round the fire when the wind is right and the chimney draws, in the kitchen the stone flags lead to a hearth wide and cold as a Druid altar, where peats smoulder as they stand on end, and hiss with raindrops in the chimney. You can make a chart of the winds and currents that eddy into unlikely corners and eventually wind into your spine. A wooden settle with high back and sides usually wards off the worst of the cold; and here my father would take his wet shoes off with a crowd of spaniels clustering about him, before he went into the tidy part of the house, where my mother was being acclimatised: for when he married her, he rented a lodging in a Dartmoor farm called Berrydown, and brought her there from her Italian home.

At seventeen, my mother was tall, with red-gold curls and the dark inherited eyebrows; a gay, irregular and wilful mouth, and a mind and body both brilliant and alluring. I have met people who knew her at this time and spoke of her as a sort of Diana, a vision of radiance. Even the grocer at Chagford, many years afterwards, told me that 'it was always a pleasure when your mother came to buy things, miss: she was a lady full of life: she made everything look bright when she came'. The splendid presence, the buoyant confidence, were her charm.

Unlike my grandmother, she was never able to build herself an 'island of desire' away from the actual world, but lived without introspection, in every moment as it came. In the course of her long life I think she never realised what light and shadow of love come to most women in their youth. My father, eight years older, unobtrusively, inarticulately tender, was so deeply observant of her freedom and his own (he would not coerce even a plant or animal out of its natural path) that she took him for granted, and knew as little of him as she did of the sights and secrets of the country, which bored her to exasperation. I remember being surprised many years later to discover that she had no idea of the connection between a hazel tree and a catkin after living for years in a part of the country where hazels are the background of every copse.

The unexpectedness of life, waiting round every corner, catches even wise women unaware. To avoid corners altogether is, after all, to refuse to live. But most people learn by experience what may be coming; they keep themselves elastic, so as to swerve a little to left or right if an obstacle appears, and adapt their contours in some degree to the asperities of the surrounding world. My mother never thought of doing this. It was no strength in her, for she was uncertain of her direction and inclined to adopt the most promiscuous guidance as it came: but she could not realise that the object in the middle of her path was an obstacle, and would throw herself against it as I have seen horses (unreasonable animals) fling themselves against a van or doorway when blinded by some fright or fancy of their own. Just so, and with the same reaction of baffled injury, my mother flung herself against the adverse facts of life, and never I think, to the end of her days, understood how easy it would have been to circumvent them.

According to Dr Johnson, it is 'so far from natural to a man and woman to live in a state of marriage, that we find all the motives they have for remaining in that connection, and the restraints which civilised society imposes to prevent separation, are hardly sufficient to keep them together'. The Victorians thought to manage it through a hierarchy of subjection, taking the Church as their analogy for wedlock – and a good many men still like to think of their wives as they do of their religion, neglected but always there. But the Church admits a short-cut to God for which the Victorian marriage provided no equivalent. A family hierarchy only works when unofficial relief is recognised and unofficial love, however tacitly, is allowed. To presume to carve up the human variety into parents and children, husbands and wives, and to cover these huge categories with a few general attributes to which every individual among them must conform; and then to make sin of all deviation – it is as if one parcelled the air and expected the plants to breathe in tight compartments, regardless of their roots. In such a dispensation, the feeble shrub may suffocate and die, but the tree will take its space and grow its height regardless, drawing its nourishment unseen as does the human soul; and only the most fearful unhappiness or perversion can come out of any *rigid* tampering with the particularism of nature.

My mother came to England singularly ill-equipped to deal with the Victorian order so uncompromisingly superimposed on the untidiness of God. Life in the Florence villa had practically not been domestic at all; and my grandmother's remoteness, buried in

Gregorovius,[1] and the unattractiveness of the German governess made any ordinary relationships of men and women more or less invisible there. She had seen no society except as a child before her father's death, and had never been to England; and now arrived like a young barbarian into the most stodgy, little-town, middle-class atmosphere that had ever been in the world.

Half the marriages that go wrong are destroyed by too much amiability at the outset; each human being has things that in the long run he cannot assimilate or forgo – and to try to do so only means a slow accumulation of disaster. It is far better to know the limits of one's resistance at once and put up as it were a little friendly fence around the private ground. Though un-Victorian, this would have been easy enough with my father, who was far too real and humble ever to wish to dominate another creature; but both were guileless and young, docile and honest, and the assumptions of their time destroyed them. My mother tried perseveringly to believe that marriage was for duty and not pleasure; my father demanded nothing, but took it all as a stability of nature rather than the false-solid façade of men, and continued to love in silence, never looking at another woman all the length of his life: and after many years, during which my sister and I grew up as it were in shadow, the human roots did their work underground, out of sight, out of consciousness even, and my mother's life shot out into its own sunlight, respectable but eccentric, and devastating to most of the lives around her.

This was all in the future, but the fact that I knew later times, and sadder memories, may have added a

[1] nineteenth-century German historian

sober colour to my picture of the early years: to my mother's description for instance of the Dartmoor weather as it appeared to one accustomed to the delicate lights of the Tuscan hills. After three days of the unbroken south-west wind, when she had ridden or walked morning and afternoon, and had been soaked every time, and there were no more dry tweeds left in the house to wear, my father (who went out undeterred) came home to her in the middle of the fourth day to find the whole house shuttered up, the lamps and candles lit, and my mother savagely reading, trying to forget the existence of a climate.

The stolidity and dreariness of conversation chilled her in the same way. She told me how, at a first 'county' dinner party to which she was invited as a bride, she moved her hand suddenly – probably with one of those swift deplorably foreign gestures – and upset her wineglass. Of the eighteen people at the table no one spoke, while the little red stream spread and died among the begonias. In Italy they would have laughed.

It was a cold world, and a later generation would have eased it by allowing her to work or to travel: but such an idea never occurred to the solid middle class of the 1880s; and there was the further complication that she had no penny of her own. My father helped her to settle her parents' affairs in Florence with generosity so natural to him and so quiet that everyone else took it for granted as he did. He was partly supporting my Florence grandmother, as he continued to do for the rest of her life, and was paying for a younger sister's education at school. It never occurred to him that my mother would like pocket money of her own, and no one had suggested a settlement at the time of the wedding; the necessity of asking for every trifle entered with extraordinary bitterness into my mother's

43

memory, so that her chief desire in later times was to earn enough to pay independently for herself. The fact that even a housekeeper is entitled to a livelihood never comforted her: she felt dependent and loathed it: and the intensity of this feeling was so borne in upon me that it has left me with a complex about money in family life, so that I would always keep it clear-cut, businesslike and apart, to prevent it from intruding on feelings which it so easily destroys.

My father was very difficult over money. He would for instance gladly take us down the High Street of Torquay to buy boots which were good for bogs and kept the water out: a party frock when required was another matter and demanded weeks of diplomacy; and my mother's exasperation was not lessened when – in the very midst of remarks about extravagance – he would come home delighted with some new, small, and to her quite uninteresting daffodil or rhododendron, for which he had paid as much as would have kept her happy for a month.

She had, I think, a wrong idea, that came from the pride of her nature and a love of giving which was passionate. She was not feminine under this aspect, and lacked the wisdom of women, the receptive, listening wisdom, which is their part in nature and in birth. Not command and obedience, but giving and receiving makes the duet of male and female, and I believe there is something psychologically sound in the tribal habit of piling the family substance in bracelets and necklaces and anklets about the person of the woman in the home. The giving of gifts is a symbol of the profounder relationship; it is no empty prejudice that makes the gifts of a man to a woman more harmonious than those of a woman to a man. The Victorian reduction of all to a property basis has dimmed the fundamental relation;

and even maternity, in which other generations saw the angelic messenger, the accepting virgin, is now contemplated, as is the whole life of women, in its most active light. The *dignity* of receiving, smirched and made sordid in the industrial age, has been forgotten.

To my mother it was radically antagonistic. It was an effort to her to accept anything even from those whom she cared for most. I think she was never sufficiently in love (even in the first few years) to fuse her universe and see the relations of things to each other in a light which transcends them: she was constantly being held up by their *separateness*, and her delight was to get everything into her own hands and give it away. Apart from base grabbing, love alone makes us happily receptive, and I suppose it was because she had never really been in harmony with my father that she found it difficult to understand the shy gentleness behind his gifts. Even a dog will bring some treasured useless object and lay it with endearing feelings at one's feet. Who would not be touched and softened? Yet I have read a description by Jane Carlyle, of a brown dressing-gown with spots, an obvious horror, bought for her birthday and received with not one scrap of tenderness, but coldly on its defects alone. My mother was the opposite of heartless, but her feeling of dependence turned my father's presents almost into injuries. He would train the best horse for her with a care he did not lavish on his own. He would buy hunting crops, saddles and bridles, new palettes and brushes – all the things in his world he could think of as desirable. Later on, when my sister and I began to grow, these strange gifts so carefully thought out would come to us also at Christmases and birthdays, and I still handle some of them as if they had a bloom upon them, a never-fading freshness of affection. To my mother this double life of inanimate objects meant nothing. On one of her birthdays my father called me and put a white bicycle pump into my hand:

'Carry it to mamma on the sofa,' he said. 'Perhaps she will take it from you.'

Yet there must have been many days when they were young and happy together on the moors, though only faint echoes come down from the thirteen years of marriage which passed before I was born. Long after-wards – turning things out of an old trunk in an attic, the sort of trunk that stood high, with a rounded lid strengthened with thick splints, shackled with locks, studded with nails, the indestructible Victorian trunk, too solid for what we now have left to put inside it – opening this trunk, I came upon my mother's riding habit, dark green with a long draped skirt, and many curving seams to model her fine young breasts, and collar and cuffs of velvet.

Copenhagen

from *Neither Here nor There*

by Bill Bryson

Bill Bryson is travelling through Europe, and has now left
Germany for Denmark.

I took a train to Copenhagen. I like travelling by train
in Denmark because you are forever getting on and off
ferries. It takes longer, but it's more fun. I don't know
how anyone could fail to experience that frisson of
excitement that comes with pulling up alongside a vast
white ship that is about to sail away with you aboard it. I
grew up a thousand miles from the nearest ocean, so
for me any sea voyage, however brief, remains a novelty.
But I noticed that even the Danes and Germans, for
whom this must be routine, were peering out of the
windows with an air of expectancy as we reached the
docks at Puttgarden and our train was shunted on to
the ferry, the *Karl Carstens*.

Here's a tip for you if you ever travel on a
Scandinavian ferry. Don't be the first off the train,
because everyone will follow you, trusting you to find
the way into the main part of the ship. I was in a group
of about 300 people following a flustered man in a grey
trilby who led us on a two-mile hike around the cargo
deck, taking us up and down long avenues of railway
carriages and huge canvas-sided trucks, casting irritated
glances back at us as if he wished we would just go away,
but we knew that our only hope was to stick to him like
glue and, sure enough, he eventually found a red

button on the wall, which when pressed opened a secret hatch to the stairwell.

Overcome with new frissons of excitement, everyone clambered hurriedly up the metal stairs and made straight for the buffet. You could tell the nationality of the people by what they went for. The Germans all had plates piled high with meat and potatoes, the Danes had Carlsbergs and cream cakes, the Swedes one piece of Ryvita with a little dead fish on it. The queues were too much for me, so I went up on the top deck and stood out in the sunshine and gusty breeze as the boat cast off and, with a sound oddly like a washing machine on its first cycle, headed across the twelve miles of white-capped water between northern Germany and the Danish island of Lolland. There were about eight of us, all men, standing in the stiff breeze, pretending we weren't perishing. Slowly Puttgarden receded behind us in a wake of foam and before long Lolland appeared over the horizon and began to glide towards us, like a huge low-lying sea monster.

You cannot beat sea travel, if you ask me, but there's not much of it left these days. Even now grand plans are under way to run bridges or tunnels between all the main islands of Denmark and between Copenhagen and Sweden, and even across this stretch of water between Puttgarden and Rödbyhavn, so that people will be able to zip across it in ten minutes and scarcely notice that they have moved from one country to another. This new European impulse to blur the boundaries between countries seems a mite misguided to me.

At Rödbyhavn, our frissons spent, we all reboarded the train and rode listlessly through the rest of the afternoon to Copenhagen. Denmark was much neater and emptier than northern Germany had been. There were no factories as there had been in Germany and none of that farmyard clutter of abandoned tractors and rusting implements that you see in Belgium and Holland. Big electricity-generating wind turbines, their three-bladed fans spinning sluggishly, were dotted around the low hillsides and stood in ranks in the shallow coastal bays. It was a pity, I thought with that kind of distant casualness that comes with looking at things that are already sliding from view, that they hadn't made them more attractive – like scaled-up Dutch windmills perhaps.

It seemed odd and sad that mankind could for centuries have so effortlessly graced the landscape with structures that seemed made for it – little arched bridges and stone farmhouses, churches, windmills, winding roads, hedgerows – and now appeared quite unable to do anything to the countryside that wasn't like a slap across the face. These days everything has at best a sleek utility, like the dully practical windmills slipping past with the scenery outside my train window, or else it looks cheap and temporary, like the tin sheds and concrete hangars that pass for superstores on the edge of every medium-sized town. We used to build civilisations. Now we build shopping malls.

We reached Copenhagen's central station at a little after five, but the station tourist office was already closed. Beside it stood a board with the names of thirty or so hotels and alongside each hotel was a small red light to indicate whether it was full or not. About two-thirds of the lights were lit, but there was no map to show where the hotels stood in relation to the station. I considered for a moment jotting down some of the names and addresses, but I didn't altogether trust the board and in any case the addresses were meaningless unless I could find a map of the city.

Perplexed, I turned to find a Danish bag lady clasping my forearm and addressing me in a cheerful babble. These people have an uncanny way of knowing when I hit town. They must have a newsletter or something. We wandered together through the station, I looking distractedly for a map of the city on a wall, she holding on to my arm and sharing demented confidences with me. I suppose we must have looked an odd sight. A businessman stared at us over the top of a newspaper as we wandered past. 'Blind date,' I explained confidentially, but he just kept staring.

I could find no map of the city, so I allowed the lady to accompany me to the front entrance, where I disengaged her grip and gave her some small coins of various nations. She took them and wandered off without a backward glance. I watched her go and wondered why crazy people like train and bus stations so much. It is as if it's their office ('Honey, I'm off to the station to pick through the litter bins and mumble at strangers. See you at five!'). I can never understand why they don't go to the beach or the Alps or some place more agreeable.

I went to half a dozen hotels in the immediate neighbourhood of the station and they were all full. 'Is there some reason for this?' I asked at one. 'Some convention or national holiday or something?'

'No it's always like this,' I was assured.

Am I wrong to find this exasperating? Surely it shouldn't be too much, on a continent that thrives on trade and tourism, to arrange things so that a traveller can arrive in a city in late afternoon and find a room without having to traipse around for hours like a boat person. I mean here I was, ready to spend freely in their hotels and restaurants, subsidise their museums and trams, shower them with foreign exchange and pay their extortionate VAT of twenty-two per cent, all without a quibble, and all I asked in return was a place to lay my head.

Like most things when you are looking for them, hotels were suddenly thin on the ground in Copenhagen. I walked the length of the old part of the city without luck and was about to trudge back to the station to begin again when I came across a hotel by the waterfront called the Sophie Amalienborg. It was large, clean, modern and frightfully expensive, but they could give me a single room for two nights and I took it without hesitation. I had a steamy shower and a change of clothes and hit the streets a new man.

Is there anything, apart from a really good chocolate cream pie and receiving a large, unexpected cheque in the post, to beat finding yourself at large in a foreign city on a fair spring evening, loafing along unfamiliar streets in the long shadows of a lazy sunset, pausing to gaze in shop windows or at some church or lovely square or tranquil stretch of quayside, hesitating at street corners to decide whether that cheerful and homy restaurant you will remember fondly for years is likely to lie down this street or that one? I just love it. I could spend my life arriving each evening in a new city.

You could certainly do worse than Copenhagen. It is not an especially beautiful city, but it's an endlessly appealing one. It is home to one and a half million people – a quarter of the Danish population – but it has the pace and ambience of a university town. Unlike most great cities, it is refreshingly free of any delusions of self-importance. It has no monuments to an imperial past and little to suggest that it is the capital of a country that once ruled Scandinavia. Other cities put up statues of generals and potentates. In Copenhagen they give you a little mermaid. I think that's swell.

I walked along Nyhavn, a three-block-long street with a canal in the middle filled with tall-masted ships and lined with narrow, step-gabled seventeenth- and eighteenth-century houses, looking for all the world like a piece of Amsterdam gone astray. The neighbourhood was in fact originally settled by Dutch sailors and remained the haunt of jolly tars until recent times. Even now it has a vaguely raffish air in parts – a tattoo parlour and one or two of the sort of dive bars through whose windows you expect to see Popeye and Bluto trading blows – but these are fading relics. For years, restaurateurs have been dragging Nyhavn almost forcibly upmarket and most of the places now are yuppie bars and designer restaurants, but very agreeable places for all that, since the Danes don't seem to be the least bit embarrassed about living well, which is after all how it should be.

The whole length of Nyhavn was lined with outdoor tables, with young, blond, gorgeous people drinking, eating and enjoying the unseasonably warm weather. I always wonder in Copenhagen what they do with their old people – they must put them in cellars or send them to Arizona – because everyone, without exception, is youthful, fresh-scrubbed, healthy, blond and immensely good-looking. You could cast a Pepsi commercial in Copenhagen in fifteen seconds. And they all look so happy.

The Danes are so full of joie de vivre that they practically sweat it. In a corner of Europe where the inhabitants have the most blunted concept of pleasure (in Norway, three people and a bottle of beer is a party; in Sweden the national sport is suicide), the Danes' relaxed attitude to life is not so much refreshing as astonishing. Do you know how long World War II lasted for Denmark? It was over in a day – actually less than a day. Hitler's tanks crossed the border under cover of darkness and had taken control of the country by dawn. As a politician of the time remarked, 'We were captured by telegram.' By evening they were all back in the bars and restaurants. . . .

I dined in a crowded, stylish basement restaurant half-way along Nyhavn. I was the only person who didn't look as if he had just come from the set of *Miami Vice*. All the men wore shirts buttoned to the throat and the women had big earrings and intentionally distressed hair, which they had to shove out of the way each time they went to their plate. Every one of them was beautiful. I felt like Barney Rubble. I kept expecting the manager to come to the table and say, 'Excuse me, sir, but would you mind putting some of this mousse on your hair?' In the event, the staff treated me like an old friend and the food was so superb that I didn't mind parting with the six-inch wad of banknotes that any meal in Copenhagen occasions.

When I climbed the steps to the street, darkness had fallen and the air had chilled, but people still sat outside at tables, drinking and talking enthusiastically, jackets draped over their shoulders. I crossed Kongens Nytorv, one of the city's principal squares, sleepy and green, passed beneath the soft lights of the Hotel D'Angleterre, full of yet more happy diners, and headed up Strøget, Copenhagen's main shopping street. Strøget is the world's longest pedestrian street. Actually it's five streets that run together for a little over a mile between Kongens Nytorv and the city's other main square, Raadhuspladsen, at the Tivoli end. Every travel article you read about Copenhagen talks rapturously about Strøget, but I always feel vaguely disappointed by it. Every time I see it, it seems to have grown

53

a tiny bit seedier. There are still many swish and diverting stores down at the Kongens Nytorv end – Georg Jensen for silver, Brødrene Andersen for clothes, Holmegaard for china and glass – but as you pass the half-way point Strøget swiftly deteriorates into tatty gift shops and McDonald's, Burger Kings and other brightly lit temples of grease. The whole thing could do with a lot more in the way of benches and flagstones (it's all patched asphalt now) and even – dare I say it? – the odd tub of geraniums. It's a shame that in a country as wealthy and design-conscious as Denmark they can't make the whole street – the words tumble involuntarily from my lips – more picturesque.

Still, it is pleasant to walk from one end of the downtown to the other without encountering cars, and just as you reach the western end, when you think that this is too, too dreary and you really should turn back, you step into the large and colourful Raadhuspladsen, or town hall square. One of the things they do in Europe that has always impressed me is let advertisers put colourful neon signs all over the roofs and top floors of the buildings around their main squares. You don't notice the signs in the daytime because they are so high up, so the buildings preserve that air of stern magnificence appropriate to their function, but when darkness falls and you could do with a little gaiety, the same buildings suddenly light up with bright advertisements that illuminate the square and colour the faces of the people below.

I walked across to Tivoli, even though I could see from a distance that it was shut and darkened, as if under dust sheets. A sign on the gate said it wouldn't open for a couple of weeks. As I walked back across the square towards Strøget I encountered a small crowd by the town hall and stopped to have a look.

Two police officers, a man and a woman, both young and blond and as gorgeous as everyone else in the city, were talking softly and with sympathy to a boy of about seventeen who had clearly ingested the sort of drugs that turn one's brain into an express elevator to Pluto. Disorientated by this sudden zip through the cosmos, he had apparently stumbled and cracked his head; a trickle of blood ran from above his hairline to his downy cheek. The police officers were wearing the smartest commando-style uniforms I have ever seen – navy blue jump suits with lots of zips and velcro pockets and loops holding torches and notebooks and portable telephones and, for all I know, grappling hooks and rocket launchers. They looked as if between them they could handle any contingency, from outbreaks of Lassa fever to disarming a nuclear submarine.

And the thing is, this was probably the biggest thing they would have to deal with all evening. The Danes are almost absurdly law-abiding. The most virulent crime in the country is bike theft. In 1982, a year for which I just happen to have the facts at my fingertips, there were six murders in Copenhagen, compared with 205 in Amsterdam, a city of similar size, and 1,688 in New York. The city is so safe that Queen Margarethe used to walk from Amalienborg Palace to the shops every morning to buy flowers and vegetables just like a normal citizen. I once asked a Dane who guarded her in such circumstances, and he looked at me with surprise and replied, 'Why, we all do,' which I thought was rather sweet.

The police officers helped the boy to his feet and led him to the patrol car. The small crowd dispersed, but I found myself following them, almost involuntarily. I don't know why I was so fascinated, except that I had never seen such gentle police. At the patrol car, I said in

55

English to the female officer, 'Excuse me, what will you do with the boy?'

'We'll take him home,' she said simply, then raised her eyebrows a fraction and added: 'I think he needs his bed.'

I was impressed. I couldn't help thinking of the time I was stopped by police in America, made to stand with my arms and legs spread against a wall and frisked, then taken to a police station and booked because of an unpaid parking ticket. I was about seventeen myself at the time. God knows what they would have done to me if they had found me in a drugged stupor on a city bench. I suppose I'd be getting out of jail about now. 'Will he be in trouble for this?' I asked.

'With his father, I think so, yes. But not with us. We are all young and crazy sometimes, you know? Good-night. Enjoy your stay in Copenhagen.'

'Goodnight,' I said, and with the deepest admiration watched them go.

The Rapids of the Ogowé

from *Travels in West Africa*

by Mary Kingsley

In 1895 many people tried to stop Mary Kingsley from attempting the Alemba rapids of the Ogowé river (the Ogooué, in modern Gabon, West Africa). Characteristically, however, she was determined that nothing would put her off. After battling for some days in a large canoe against the many dangers of the Ogowé with its ferocious currents, rapids and whirlpools, she and her crew, captained by M'bo, hear a new, incredible sound.

I said to M'bo: 'That's a thunderstorm away among the mountains.' 'No, sir,' says he, 'that's the Alemba.'

We paddled on towards it, hugging the right-hand bank again to avoid the mid-river rocks. For a brief space the mountain wall ceased, and a lovely scene opened before us; we seemed to be looking into the heart of the chain of the Sierra del Cristal, the abruptly shaped mountains encircling a narrow plain or valley before us, each one of them steep in slope, every one of them forest-clad; one, whose name I know not unless it be what is sometimes put down as Mt Okana on the French maps, had a conical shape which contrasted beautifully with the more irregular curves of its companions. The colour down this gap was superb, and very Japanese in the evening glow. The more distant peaks were soft grey-blues and purple, those nearer, indigo and black. We soon passed this lovely scene and entered the walled-in channel, creeping up what seemed an interminable hill of black water, then through some whirlpools and a rocky channel to the sand and rock shore of our desired island Kondo Kondo, along whose northern side tore in thunder the Alemba. We made our canoe fast in a little cove among the rocks, and landed, pretty stiff and tired and considerably damp. This island, when we were on it, must have been about half a mile or so long, but during the long wet season a good deal of it is covered, and only the higher parts – great heaps of stone, among which grows a long branched willow-like shrub – are above or nearly above water. The Adooma from Kembe Island especially drew my attention to this shrub, telling me his people who worked the rapids always regarded it with an affectionate veneration; for he said it was the only thing that helped a man when his canoe got thrown over in the dreaded Alemba, for its long tough branches swimming in, or close to, the water are veritable life lines, and his best chance; a chance which must have failed some poor fellow, whose knife and leopard-skin belt we found wedged in among the rocks on Kondo Kondo. The main part of the island is sand, with slabs and tables of polished rock sticking up through it; and in between the rocks grew in thousands most beautiful lilies, their white flowers having a very strong scent of vanilla and their bright light-green leaves looking very lovely on the glistening pale sand among the black-grey rock. How they stand the long submersion they must undergo I do not know; the natives tell me they begin to spring up as soon as ever the water falls and leaves the island exposed; that they very soon grow up and flower, and keep on flowering until the Ogowé comes down again and rides roughshod over Kondo Kondo for months. While the men were making their fire I went across the island to see the great

Alemba rapid, of which I had heard so much, that lay between it and the north bank. Nobler pens than mine must sing its glory and its grandeur. Its face was like nothing I have seen before. Its voice was like nothing I have heard. Those other rapids are not to be compared to it; they are wild, headstrong, and malignant enough, but the Alemba is not as they. It does not struggle, and writhe, and brawl among the rocks, but comes in a majestic springing dance, a stretch of waltzing foam, triumphant.

The beauty of the night on Kondo Kondo was superb; the sun went down and the afterglow flashed across the sky in crimson, purple, and gold, leaving it a deep violet-purple, with the great stars hanging in it like moons, until the moon herself arose, lighting the sky long before she sent her beams down on us in this valley. As she rose, the mountains hiding her face grew harder and harder in outline, and deeper and deeper black, while those opposite were just enough illumined to let one see the wefts and floating veils of blue-white mist upon them, and when at last, and for a short time only, she shone full down on the savage foam of the Alemba, she turned it into a soft silver mist. Around, on all sides flickered the fire-flies, who had come to see if our fire was not a big relation of their own, and they were the sole representatives, with ourselves, of animal life. When the moon had gone, the sky, still lit by the stars, seeming indeed to be in itself lambent, was very lovely, but it shared none of its light with us, and we sat round our fire surrounded by an utter darkness. Cold, clammy drifts of almost tangible mist encircled us; ever and again came cold faint puffs of wandering wind, weird and grim beyond description. . . .

Going down big rapids is always, everywhere, more

dangerous than coming up, because when you are coming up and a whirlpool or eddy does jam you on rocks, the current helps you off – certainly only with a view to dashing your brains out and smashing your canoe on another set of rocks it's got ready below; but for the time being it helps, and when off, you take charge and convert its plan into an incompleted fragment whereas in going down the current is against your backing off. M'bo had a series of prophetic visions as to what would happen to us on our way down, founded on reminiscence and tradition. I tried to comfort him by pointing out that, were any one of his prophecies fulfilled, it would spare our friends and relations all funeral expenses; and, unless they went and wasted their money on a memorial window, that ought to be a comfort to our well-regulated minds. M'bo did not see this, but was too good a Christian to be troubled by the disagreeable conviction that was in the minds of other members of my crew, namely, that our souls, unliberated by funeral rites from this world, would have to hover for ever over the Ogowé near the scene of our catastrophe. I own this idea was an unpleasant one – fancy having to pass the day in those caves with the bats, and then come out and wander all night in the cold mists! However, like a good many likely-looking prophecies, those of M'bo did not quite come off, and a miss is as good as a mile. Twice we had a near call, by being shot in between two pinnacle rocks, within half an inch of being fatally close to each other for us; but after some alarming scrunching sounds, and creaks from the canoe, we were shot ignominiously out down river. Several times we got on to partially sub-merged table rocks, and were unceremoniously bundled off them by the Ogowé, irritated at the hindrance we were occasioning; but we never met the rocks of M'bo's prophetic soul – that lurking, submerged needle, or knife-edge of a pinnacle rock which was to rip our canoe from stem to stern, neat and clean into two pieces.

A comic incident happened to us one evening. The canoe jammed among a clump of rocks, and out we went anyhow into the water. Fortunately, there were lots of rocks about; unfortunately, we each chose different ones to perch on; mine was exceedingly inconvenient, being a smooth pillar affair, to which it was all I and the French flag, which always accompanied me in upsets, could do to hold on. There was considerable delay in making up our party again, for the murkiness of the night only allowed each of us to see the foam which flew round our own particular rock, and the noise of the rapids made it difficult for us to interchange information regarding our own individual position and plan of action. However, owing to that weak-minded canoe swinging round broadside on to the rocks, she did not bolt down the river. When Pierre got to her she was trying to climb sideways over them, 'like a crab,' he said. We seven of us got into her – number eight we could not find and were just beginning to think the Ogowé had claimed another victim when we heard the strains of that fine hymn 'Notre port est au Ciel,' – which is a great favourite hereabouts owing to its noble tune, – coming to us above the rapids' clamour in an agonised howl. We went joyfully and picked the singer off his rock, and then dashed downwards to further dilemmas and disasters. The course we had to take coming down was different to that we took coming up. Coming up we kept as closely as might be to the most advisable bank, and dodged behind every rock we could, to profit by the shelter it afforded us from the current. Coming down, fallen-tree-fringed banks and rocks were converted from friends to foes; so we kept with all our power in the very centre of the swiftest part of the current in order to avoid them. The grandest part of the whole time was coming down, below the Alemba, where the whole great Ogowé takes a tiger-like spring for about half a mile, I should think, before it strikes a rock reef below. As you come out from among the rocks in the upper rapid it gives you – or I should perhaps confine myself to saying, it gave me – a peculiar internal sensation to see that stretch of black water, shining like a burnished sheet of metal, sloping down before one, at such an angle. All you have got to do is to keep your canoe-head straight – quite straight, you understand – for any failure so to do will land you the other side of the tomb, instead of in a cheerful no-end-of-a-row with lower rapid's rocks. This lower rapid is one of the worst in the dry season; maybe it is so in the wet too, for the river's channel here turns an elbow-sharp curve which infuriates the Ogowé in a most dangerous manner.

I hope to see the Ogowé next time in the wet season – there must be several more of these great sheets of water then over what are rocky rapids now. Just think what coming down over that ridge above Boko Boko will be like! I do not fancy however it would ever be possible to get up the river when it is at its height, with so small a crew as we were when we went and played our knock-about farce, before King Death, in his amphitheatre in the Sierra del Cristal.

Resisting Temptation

from *Two against the Ice*

by Ejnar Mikkelsen

It is 1910. Ejnar Mikkelsen and Iver Iversen have waited and waited for a ship to take them home after their Greenland expedition has finished. Now there is nothing left to do but walk on and try to take care of themselves.

Now and again . . . hunger did come to the surface and drive all other sensations from our consciousness: we felt it then as a physical pain, an overwhelming desire for food.

Again Iver came up alongside me, and for some minutes we walked in silence close together, swaying on our feet, stumbling and bumping shoulders; it was impossible to continue like that. 'Either behind or in front, Iver, I don't mind which; but we can't walk close together, however much we would like to.'

Iver dropped behind and I could hear his unsteady footsteps on the frozen ground, his occasional stumbles over a stone, his grunts when the pain became too great to be borne in silence. Then there he was alongside me again.

When this had happened several times, I halted and we sat down on a stone.

'What is it Iver?' I asked. 'Is it the valley again?'

He did not say much. He just sat and stared out into the distance and shook his head: 'No,' he said, 'it isn't the valley. I'm famished, I can't do much more.'

I too was famished and not able to do much more;

but there was nothing to be done about it. We had food in Danmarks Havn and there was no chance of anything edible before that, unless we ran into a bear and could shoot it.

Shoot? I looked at Iver, who was carrying the rifle, and a thought came into my head: 'Tell me honestly, Iver: is it the rifle you are afraid of?'

He nodded despairingly, looked at me steadily and held out the rifle: 'Take it and give me something of yours to carry. I can't have the rifle any longer – it's dangerous.'

So then I knew, and I refused to carry the rifle: 'Keep it, Iver,' I said, 'carry it as you have been doing and don't think too much. But if it will help your peace of mind, I can tell you that I see you in front of me the whole time. And when hunger dulls pain, weariness and reason, my thoughts are no doubt the same as yours: if he should drop and die, what then? Will you, or won't you, eat a bit of what is no longer Iver?'

Iver nodded assent and said: 'Yes, but I've got the rifle.'

'I know that, Iver,' I said. 'But keep it. After all our struggles we can walk on together, till we can walk no farther; and we can struggle on together, till we can struggle no more – or have come to our journey's end.'

The *Titanic*

by Terry Coleman

In Southampton, on the morning of 10 April 1912, a giant of a
ship left with 2,235 passengers and crew for New York. As it
sailed majestically across the bay, a steamer was sucked into its
tremendous wake and everyone watching was enthralled as
the able commander ordered a touch ahead on the port
engine, gently washing the little steamer back to safety. The
Titanic was the size of a cathedral, it had the luxury of the
finest hotels – it was the wonder of the world, and it was
thought to be unsinkable.

From Thursday noon to Friday noon the *Titanic* ran 386
nautical miles. Friday to Saturday 519 miles, and
Saturday to Sunday 546 miles. She was making 22 knots.
Everyone agreed she was the most comfortable ship
they had travelled in. There was, though, a vibration,
which was most noticeable as one lay in the bath. The
throb of the engines came straight up from the floor
through the metal sides of the tub so that one could not
put one's head back with any comfort. Throughout her
voyage, the *Titanic* slightly listed to port, but it was
nothing. As the second-class passengers sat at table in
the dining-room they could, if they watched the skyline
through the portholes, see both skyline and sea on the
port side but only sky to starboard. The purser thought
this was probably because more coal had been used
from the starboard bunkers.

When some passengers went on deck on Sunday

morning they found the temperature had dropped so rapidly that they did not care to stay outside, although there was no wind, or only that artificial wind created by the passage of the ship. Both the French liner *Touraine* and the German *Amerika* had wirelessed the *Titanic* reporting ice, and the *Titanic* had replied thanking them. Sunday dinner was served, and then coffee. Thomas Andrews, the shipbuilder, strolled down to the kitchens to thank the baker for making some special bread for him. The passengers went to bed with the presumption, perhaps already mentally half-realised, as (Lawrence) Beesley put it, that they would be ashore in New York in forty-eight hours time. At the evening service, after coffee, Rev. Mr Carter had caused the hymn 'For Those in Peril on the Sea' to be sung, but he had brought the service to a close with a few words on the great confidence all on board felt in the *Titanic*'s great steadiness and size. At 11.40, in Lat. 41° 46' N. Long. 50° 14' W. Frederick Fleet, the look-out in the crow's-nest, saw or sensed an iceberg ahead. The *Titanic* veered to port, so that it was her starboard plates which were glanced open. The engines were stopped. There was a perfectly still atmosphere. It was a brilliantly starlit night but with no moon, so that there was little light that was of any use. She was a ship that had come quietly to rest without any indication of disaster. No ice was visible: the iceberg had been glimpsed by the look-out and then gone. There was no hole in the ship's side through which water could be seen to be pouring, nothing out of place, no sound of alarm, no panic, and no movement of anyone except at a walking pace.

Within ten minutes the water had risen fourteen feet inside the ship. Mail bags were floating about in the mail room. The passengers had no idea of danger. Beesley, who was in bed, noticed no more than what he took to be the slightest extra heave of the engines. What most people noticed first was the sudden lack of engine vibration. This had been with them so constantly for the four days of the voyage that they had ceased to be conscious of it, but when it stopped they noticed the supervening silence and stillness. The only passengers who saw an iceberg were a few still playing cards in the smoking room. They idly discussed how high it might have been, settled on an estimate of eighty feet, and went back to their cards. One pointed to a glass of whisky at his side and, turning to an onlooker, suggested he should just run along on deck to see if any ice had come on board. If so, he would like some more in his whisky. They laughed. In fact, as the crew discovered, the decks were strewn with ice, but even then, so unaware were they of danger, that Edward Buley, an able seaman, picked up a handful of it, took it down to his bunk, and turned in again. There was no panic because there was no awareness. The *Titanic* was assumed to be unsinkable. The shipbuilders had said so. Practically everyone believed she was as unsinkable as a railway station. A Rothschild, asked to put on his life-jacket, said he did not think there was any occasion for it, and walked leisurely away. Stewards rode bicycles round and round in the gym. She was in fact sinking very fast, and by midnight was a quarter sunk already. There was something unusual about the stairs, a curious sense of something out of balance, a sense of not being able to put one's foot down in the right place. The stairs were tilting forward and tended to throw your feet out of place. There was no visible slope, just something strange perceived by the sense of balance. The *Titanic* was settling by the head.

There is going to be no coherent account of what

happened in the last hour of the *Titanic*, because nothing coherent happened. The *Titanic* was a sixth of a mile long and had eleven decks. What happened in one place did not happen in another. What happened on the starboard side did not happen on the port. On the port side, women and children only were allowed into the boats which were even sent away half-empty when there were not women enough at that moment to fill them, although there were men. On the starboard side, men were allowed to enter the boats when there were not at any given moment enough women to fill them. There was even a difference of opinion as to what constituted a woman. Second Officer Lightoller took any women, except stewardesses. Fifth Officer Lowe accepted any women, 'whether first class, second class, third class, or sixty-seventh class . . . regardless of class or nationality or pedigree. Stewardesses just the same.' Lowe, however, said he fended off a lot of Italian men, Latin people, all along the ship's rails, 'more or less like wild beasts, ready to spring'. But the severe Lightoller saw none of this, and said that the men whom he refused to allow into his boats 'could not have stood quieter if they had been in church'. Major Arthur Peuchen, who held his commission in the Canadian militia and got away into a boat because he was a yachtsman and could help to handle it, saw a hundred stokers with their bags crowd a whole deck in front of the boats until an officer he did not recognise, a very powerful man, drove them right off the deck like a lot of sheep. Others said not a soul emerged from the engine room. Certainly no single engineer survived. Lowe said they were never seen.

Everyone agrees that the band played until the last. There were eight of them, and none survived. They had played throughout dinner and then gone to their berths. About twenty to one, when the ship was foundering, the cellist ran down the deserted starboard deck, his cello trailing behind him with the spike dragging along the floor. Soon after that the band began to play ragtime. They were still playing ragtime when the last boat was launched.

Colonel Astor, having placed his young bride in one of the boats, lit a cigarette and looked over the rails. Benjamin Guggenheim changed into evening dress, saying that if he had to die he would die like a gentleman. Thomas Andrews leaned against a mantelpiece in the smoking room. A steward asked him, 'Aren't you going to try for it, sir?' He did not reply. John Collins, aged seventeen, an assistant cook making his first sea voyage, saw the stewards with their white jackets steering some passengers along, making a joke of it. One steward was helping a woman with two children. The steward was carrying one child and the woman the other. Collins took the child the woman was carrying. 'Then,' he said, 'the sailors and the firemen that were forward seen the ship's bow in the water and seen that she was intending to sink her bow, and they shouted out for all they were worth we were to go aft, and we were just turning round and making for the stern when the wave washed us off the deck, washed us clear of it, and the child was washed out of my arms: and the wreckage, and the people that was around me, they kept me down for at least two or three minutes under the water.' The sea was calm as a board, but when the bow went under the water it created a wave that washed the decks clear, and there were hundreds on it.

These are the detailed figures for survivors given in the report of the British Board of Trade Inquiry:

	Number on board	Number saved	Percentage saved
First-class passengers			
Men	173	58	34
Women	144	139	97
Children	5	5	100
Second-class passengers			
Men	160	13	8
Women	93	78	84
Children	24	24	100
Third-class passengers			
Men	454	55	12
Women	179	98	55
Children	76	23	30
Total passengers	1308	493	38
Crew	898	210	23
Total	2206	703	32

Taking each class of passenger as a whole, of the first class 63 per cent were saved, of the second class 42 per cent, and of the third class 23 per cent.

Beyond the Golden Road

by Michelle MacGrath

While living in Russia, Michelle MacGrath travels with friends
to Uzbekistan, then the largest province in Soviet Asia. They
reach Bukhara.

As we drew near to the market we could see what
appeared to be a huge yellow carpet, shading here and
there into green, spread out before the high market
building. Closer still, we discovered this apparently
solid mass consisted of countless torpedo-shaped
melons laid in rows under the nonchalant eye of an old,
bearded Uzbek chatting to a friend. At fifty or sixty
kopecks a kilo, both green and yellow melons are some
of the most succulent you can find, only a few of the
thousand different varieties grown in the republic.
Inside the covered market the abundance of fruit and
vegetables was no less great: pomegranates, grapes,
apples and pears, mountains of radishes, pale carrots,
potatoes, turnips, delicate lettuces, parsley and dill,
hills of white and brown beans, lentils, raisins, sultanas,
walnuts and soft dried apricots. A multitude of colours.
The air was fresh, a turbulent current of earthy frag-
rances and purposeful activity.

The grey October afternoon dissolved into drizzle as
we stood facing the imposing portal of the seventeenth-
century Abdulaziz-Khan Medresseh. Our backs to the
fifteenth-century Ulug Beg Medresseh with its niche-
like windows and inspiring inscription, 'It is the duty of

71

every true Muslim, man and woman, to strive after knowledge', we observed a teatime scene. A group of seven or eight young boys, their faces held in rapt attention, were aiming stones at a strategically positioned briefcase. A ragged procession of children passed by in the delightful freedom of the close of school. In twos and threes they dawdled along, clutching bags and satchels, engrossed in conversation. One lone little girl slowed down to wriggle deftly out of her white pinafore. Wiping her nose on it without the least concern, she thrust it deep into her bag and continued on her way, her every movement a sigh of relief.

A weary donkey plodded slowly by before a rickety cart calmly driven by an old man in a fur hat, sadly bedraggled by the rain, and a quilted black coat tied at the waist with a blue striped cloth. A group of Russian tourists on a trip round some of the other Soviet republics stood out against the darker complexions and Asiatic features of the native Uzbeks. The group paused for a few minutes in front of the two *medressehs'* dramatic façades as the guide's flow of information was suddenly engulfed in the aggressive roar of a motor bike and the persistent clanging of an iron-wheeled cart trundling leisurely along. Another old man shuffled painfully past, his frail back bowed down by a huge sack of potatoes, his black coat bound with a dark pink scarf, a white cloth around his *tyubeteika* gave a turban effect. Two teenage girls came into view, sauntering cheerfully along arm in arm. With their bright loose trousers, contrasting dresses and patterned shawls and their long, thick, black hair, they were two patches of living colour set against the subdued tones of the streets. Behind them appeared three assertive young men in the dark trousers, white shirts and embroidered *tyubeteikas* that are so typical for young men of their age.

We stood long in the street between the two *medressehs* and watched the exotic and the familiarly Universal drift slowly by.

'No seats,' came the answer from the airport.

'No seats,' the man at the hotel service desk affirmed indifferently.

'But we have to get to Samarkand. We have a flight from there back to Moscow the day after tomorrow. Isn't there a train or a bus or something?'

'The railway's inconvenient, a long way from the town, but there are coaches.'

'Where do they leave from? Is it far?'

'No. They go from the coach station. A number 7 bus will take you there. The stop's just outside the hotel.'

We left in the direction indicated and found an incognito bus stop in what appeared to be the correct spot. We asked one of the five or six Uzbeks already waiting if this was the right stop for the coach station.

'Yes, indeed,' the woman, who looked in her late fifties, replied. 'Are you from Moscow? What do you think of our city?'

'Oh, it's really beautiful. So peaceful.'

'Much better than Moscow. Grapes are four or five roubles a kilo there, but they're only fifty kopecks here!'

We nodded and smiled at this irrefutable argument clinching Bukhara's superiority over the capital. The woman was pleased and, delving into her string shopping bag, proudly presented us with a blushing pomegranate.

'Here, have this from our Uzbek soil.'

We thanked her and waited. The queue swelled, but no bus arrived. Some twenty minutes later an empty and obviously off-duty bus swung innocently into the street to be flagged down immediately by an energetic member of the queue. A brief conversation in Uzbek ensued and then everyone climbed aboard. We quickly followed suit and drove happily in our hijacked bus to the coach station on the other side of town. A crowd of people, some in Western dress and others in traditional Uzbek trousers and thick padded coats, stood studying the timetable. A host of coaches connects the city with the towns and the state and collective farms in the area since plane and bus are the major means of transport. Although three-fifths of Uzbekistan is desert, extensive irrigation has made much of it fertile and it is now an important region for fruit growing, viticulture and cotton. We had seen from the air the vegetation clinging along the river valleys and irrigation canals and creeping gradually but persistently out into the dull sands of the desert.

Twelve hours driving takes you to the capital, Tashkent. In six hours twenty minutes and for as little as five roubles seventy-five kopecks you can cover the 272 kilometres to Samarkand. We took two tickets for the following afternoon.

Our last memory of Bukhara was therefore that of the patient crowds in the busy forecourt of the coach station. With a handful of locals we climbed aboard a smart red and white coach and left on time to speed along the desert roads which run arrowlike for kilometres before abruptly changing direction in inexplicably acute bends. We stopped occasionally in the crowded bus station yard of some small town and watched for a while the ebb and flow of the rush-hour throng: the local cafe beseiged, the crowds milling aimlessly awaiting a bus to go home.

In the dying daylight we drove past clusters of low houses that lie baking for eight months a year in temperatures of 40°C and freeze in winter with the thermometer sometimes dropping to −25°C, and past small reservoirs shaded by a fringe of tall trees. We glimpsed a collage of life as the road threaded on through the valley of the river Zeravsham, 'the bestower of gold', so called because its waters irrigate the land and make it rich. We caught swift images of donkeys and carts, of children playing, of bent figures at work in the fields, and of the soft white stacks of harvested cotton rising up like mountains in the towns.

Darkness fell quickly and it was in the black of a southern night that we arrived back in Samarkand. From the magic of one city we had returned to the power of the other, and only the desert held the two spells apart.

The First Contest

from *Unreasonable Behaviour*

by Don McCullin

The photojournalist Don McCullin has been sent to Cyprus in the early 1960s by the *Observer*. A civil war is raging between the Greeks and the Turks who share this Mediterranean island. McCullin is driving through Limassol with a colleague from the newspaper when they hear the sound of guns firing.

It was late in the afternoon, and we were deep in the Turkish quarter. I said to Ivan, 'I want to stay here because it looks as if this is going to be it.'

I drove out to get Ivan a cab, and then came back to the same spot. As I parked the car, I saw a group of men with weapons crouched in the road. They wore old long British greatcoats and balaclava helmets. I went up and asked for the police station. They jumped on me, and I reached the police station under close arrest, with Turkish escort. After some hours of questioning the police released me and in the middle of the night took me to what had been a community centre and was now converted, because of the hostilities, into a hospital.

After some fitful sleep, I was woken early by a clanging noise. It proved to be a bullet hitting the iron grille of the window behind which I had been sleeping. Then it started in earnest and the firing grew heavier and heavier. The intensity of that hail of bullets was greater than anything I was prepared for. The reality of firepower exceeds almost anything that Hollywood dares to offer.

I was shaking with a combination of awe, fear and a kind of excitement. Though it wasn't clear at the time, what had happened was that some 5,000 armed Greek irregulars had furtively surrounded this small Turkish quarter of Limassol and opened fire from corners and rooftops. The Turkish community had withdrawn for safety into communal buildings, and the Turks were mounting a counter-attack.

I went out into the middle of this gun battle and took shelter behind an armoured car, wrongly thinking it would give me protection. From this vantage point I took the picture that later aroused much comment – of a Turkish gunman emerging at a run, his shadow sharply defined on a wall. I took risks that later I would never have taken. I was determined to face up to fear and defy it. As the battle moved I ran here, there and everywhere. I was wound up to an extreme pitch, feeling completely surrounded by this onslaught and weighted down with the responsibility of being the only pressman there to record what was going on and to convey it to the world. I ran from street to street, trying not to miss one significant thing, trying to get as close as possible, to carry myself into situations where reporters, and especially reporters with cameras, were never meant to be. Some shots I took when I was in the direct firing line of snipers.

It was a kind of madness. The battle lasted all day, and I felt I had lived a lifetime. In one street I saw a cinema, into which families had been put for safety, come under heavy fire. I saw people stumbling into the battle as you and I might do, going round the corner to the local shops. Some couldn't register what was going on. An old woman got caught up in the crossfire, and fell. An old man, I suppose her husband, came out to help her, as though she had slipped with her shopping basket. She lay in a pool of her own blood, and he fell beside her from the same sniper bullets.

I saw women running with mattresses over their heads for protection from the bullets, as they might put on scarves to keep off rain.

I watched horrified as, under the duress of fire, one of the buildings disgorged its Turkish defenders and its occupants. Women and children also began to appear. I remember putting my cameras down and belting across the fire-field to retrieve a three-year-old whose mother was screaming, and carrying it to safety. In later years I would develop a principle about trying to put back into a situation from which I was taking. But there was no theory at work that day. It was all instinct.

Part of the cause of the Cyprus conflict, I sensed – and I tried to capture it in that picture of the gunman – was nothing more than the Eastern Mediterranean, moustachioed, half-bandit undercurrent of vendetta, or what people called machismo. This touchy masculine pride and honour, pride in aggression and revenge, instantaneous reaction to a situation in which there were for the combatants only black and white, only emotional certainties, no grey questionable areas or matters calling for deliberation or understanding, was all acted out in the fierce heat of the sun.

Yet what remains with me even more strongly than that gun battle is my first quiet encounter with the carnage of war. It took place in a little Turkish village of stone and mud called Ayios Sozomenos, about 15 miles from Nicosia. It was very still as I got out of my car on the village outskirts and saw shepherds herding their flocks away. I photographed an attractive young girl of about eighteen wearing a headscarf and carrying a double-barrelled shotgun. She held her head high as she was solemnly walking away. I could hear distant crying. And I could smell burning. I could sense there was death around. I heard voices and went towards them up a rise in the ground. Some British soldiers were standing by an armoured vehicle. I went up and said 'Aye, aye' as if I'd seen them after a country walk in Somerset.

'Morning,' one of the soldiers said. 'Want to see a dead body, mate? There's one over there. Been hit in the face with a shotgun. Not very pleasant.'

I thought, O Christ, am I going to be able to handle it?

I came to this man's feet, which were splayed, and my eyes travelled up the length of his body to the face – what was left of it. I could see the dark brown eyes fixed in a stare, as if looking at the sky. I thought back to my father's death. I thought, This is what it's like. I thought, It is bad, but it's not too bad for me to bear.

As I walked away the soldier said, 'Oh, there's two more in that house.'

I went to the stone house and knocked on the window. There was silence. I turned the handle and opened the door. The early morning cold syphoned out warm sticky air. It was a sticky carnage that I saw. The floor was covered with blood. A man was lying on his face, another flat on his back. There wasn't a mark on him, or seemed to be none. There was no sound. I let myself in and closed the door. I could smell something burning. In another room I found a third man dead. Three men dead, a father and two sons, one in his early twenties, the other slightly older.

Suddenly the door opened and people came in led by what I later learned was the wife of the youngest man. They had been married only a few days. All the presents were laid out in the front room, all shot up in the gun battle. Broken cups and saucers, glass objects and ornaments, brought as gifts to the wedding.

I'm in serious trouble now, I thought. They will think I have trespassed in their house. I had already taken photographs. It wasn't just trespass in the legal sense I had been guilty of, for I had trespassed on death, and emotion too. The woman picked up a towel to cover her husband's face and started to cry.

I remember saying something awkward like – forgive me, I'm from a newspaper, and I cannot believe what I'm looking at.

I pointed to my hand with the camera in it, asking for an invitation to record the tragedy. An older man said, 'Take your pictures, take your pictures.' They *wanted* me to do it. I was to discover that all Middle Eastern people want to express and record their grief. Grief is something they express very vividly. It's not just the Turks and Greeks, but a Mediterranean thing, a very outward display of mourning.

When I realised I had been given the go-ahead to photograph, I started composing my pictures in a very serious and dignified way. It was the first time I had pictured something of this immense significance and I felt as if I had a canvas in front of me and I was, stroke by stroke, applying the composition to a story that was telling itself. I was, I realised later, trying to photograph in a way that Goya painted or did his war sketches.

Eventually, the woman knelt down by the side of her young husband and cradled his head. I was very young then, and I knew that pain, and I found it hard not to burst into tears. When I walked out of the house I was shattered. I was dehydrated. My mouth was glued together.

I think I grew up that day. I took a step away from my personal resentments, my feeling that life had been uniquely tough on me, giving me evacuation and Finsbury Park, and taking away my father when I was young. That day in Cyprus, when I saw somebody else losing their father, somebody else losing their son, I felt I could somehow assimilate this experience so that my own pity could cease to be personal and instead become general. And I could just say 'OK. I'm not the only one.'

The next day, in another village, I photographed the family of a Turkish shepherd who had been shot in the hills. The poor shepherds were the soft targets of course. They were preparing a makeshift coffin and the dead shepherd's son was looking on, a young boy of about the age I was when they brought my own father's body back from the hospital. With a curious ceremonial dignity they offered me the bullet that had passed through the shepherd's body. Experiences like this were an ordeal, but I also felt as if they were a privilege. In an inexplicable way they were teaching me how to become a human being.

Cyprus left me with the beginnings of a self-knowledge, and the very beginning of what they call empathy. I found I was able to share other people's emotional experiences, live with them silently, transmit them. I felt I had a particular vision that isolated and homed in on the essence of what was happening, and could see that essence in light, in tones, in details. That I had a powerful ability to communicate.

What I hoped I had captured in my pictures was an enduring image that would imprint itself on the world's memory. I was looking for a symbol – though I could not then have put it that way – that could stand for the whole story and would have the impact of ritual or religious imagery.

Desert Rains

from *Arabian Sands*

by Wilfred Thesiger

Wilfred Thesiger and his Bedu travelling companions have been in desert rains for seven days and nights. During his years in southern Arabia (1945–50) he has shared the hunger and thirst that is their daily lot, and endured with them the intense heat in summer and the freezing nights of winter. The rain is an added torment.

They were miserable days. It was maddening to ride along drenched to the skin and watch the driving rain soak into the sand, for although I was bitterly cold I was also thirsty. We had no idea where we should find more water, and were again rationing ourselves to a pint a day. We had nothing with us, except a few small pots, in which to catch the rain, not that we could afford the time to stop. My companions were worried about the camels, and warned me that we might wake up any morning and find some of them dead, killed in their weakened state by the ulcers which were eating into them. Each morning I looked anxiously to see if they were still alive.

One night there was a terrific storm, which started soon after dark and revolved around us until dawn. On that bare plain there was no sort of shelter. We could only lie cowering on the ground while the lightning slashed through the darkness of driven clouds, and the thunder crashed about our ears. I had placed my rug and sheepskin over my sleeping-bag. On other nights these had kept me fairly dry, but tonight the weight of water was too great to be turned aside. It flowed over me like an icy torrent. Sometimes the rain stopped and I peered out to see, silhouetted against the night by the almost continuous flashes of lightning, the dark shapes where the others lay beneath their coverings, like grave-mounds on a wet seashore; and the group of sodden animals, squatting tail to storm. Then I would hear the muffled drumming of the rain as it came down once more. I was certain that some of our camels would die that night, but in the morning they were still alive.

At dawn there was no wood dry enough to light a fire. We exchanged once more the sodden misery of the night for the cold, dripping discomfort of the day, as we forced the unwilling camels forward into the wind and stinging rain. Nothing grew here but occasional matted growths of salt-bush, whose juicy green foliage gave an irritating illusion of fertility to depressions which were really more sterile than the surrounding sands. That evening the starving camels, finding nothing else, ate these bushes and suffered next day from the inevitable diarrhoea. We tied their tails sideways to our saddlery to prevent them from flicking messily over our clothes. There was no food in their stomachs, but this loss of liquid would entail immediate thirst. Luckily we came on a well, a shallow hole in hard sand, discernible from a distance only by the carpet of camel-droppings that surrounded it. We tasted the water, but it was too brackish to drink; the thirsty camels, however, drank as if they could never have enough. While we watered them a gleam of pale sunlight flooded across the wet plain, like slow, sad music. Then it started to rain again. Bin Kabina coaxed a fire to burn, and cooked a large meal of rice in water from the well, but it tasted horrible and most of it remained uneaten.

Next day was fine and sunny and our spirits rose as the sun dried our clothes and warmed our bodies. My companions sang as we rode across sands which looked as if they had been uncovered by an outgoing tide. They were Bedu and it had rained, not scattered showers, but downpours which might well have covered all the desert. 'God's bounty' they called it, and rejoiced at the prospect of rich grazing that would last for years. As I rode across these interminable naked sands it seemed incredible that in three months' time they would be covered with flowering shrubs. Eskimos enduring the cold and the darkness of the arctic winter can count the days till the sun appears, but here in southern Arabia the Bedu have no certainty of spring. Often there is no rain, and even if there is, it may fall at any time of the year. Generally the bitter winters turn to blazing summers over a parched and lifeless land. Bin Kabina told me now that he only remembered three springs in his life. Occasional springtimes such as these were all the Bedu ever knew of the gentleness of life. A few years' relief from the anxiety of want was the most they ever hoped for. It seemed to me pathetically little and yet I knew that it was magnificently enough.

As we rode along, the others spoke of years when it had rained, and bin Kabina told me that never in his life had he known such rain as this. Then inevitably they spoke of the great flood in Dhaufar of sixty years ago. I had myself seen palm-trunks which had been jammed by this flood eighteen feet up among the rocks in the cliffs of the Wadi Aidam, where the valley was more than a thousand yards wide. We speculated as to how many days it must have rained to produce this flood, which had occurred in summer when it was warm. I wondered how long a man could survive such rain in winter before he died of exposure. It rained again in the evening and continued to do so intermittently for the next three days.

On the afternoon of the eighth day since we had left Jabrin I reckoned that we must be near Dhiby well, and my calculation was confirmed by the bearings which I took on two rocky peaks in a low escarpment to the north of us. An hour later, after again checking our position, I said that we were near the well. Bin Ghabaisha went off to look for it and found it a quarter of a mile away in a hollow in the sands. He came back and said, 'By God, Umbarak, you *are* a guide!', but my justifiable satisfaction was spoilt when the water proved too brackish to drink. The camels, however, were thirsty and drank it greedily.

Near the well there was a little fresh *qassis* which I hoped foretold that we were on the edge of grazing, but the next day we marched twenty-eight miles and found nothing all day. It rained again throughout the night. I was too cold and wet to sleep, too worried about what we should do. We had decided to go on to the Sabkhat Mutti, still hoping to find Arabs, but as we had found no trace of any so far I saw no reason why we should. My map marked only Abu Dhabi about two hundred and fifty miles farther on and our water was nearly finished.

We woke to a grey, lowering day, heavy with massed clouds, threatening rain. With cold, numbed fingers we loaded our camels and then walked dispiritedly beside them trying to bring some warmth into our bodies, while our long shirts flapped damply round our legs. I felt sure that the camels could not survive another day. Then unbelievably we came on grazing. It covered only a few square miles, and we walked straight into it. The camels hardly moved. They just ate and ate. We stood and watched them and bin Ghabaisha said to me, 'This grazing has saved our lives.'

Experiences of a Pioneer Arizona Woman

by Sarah Butler York

Sarah Butler York's life as a pioneer wife in nineteenth-century America was one of hardship and danger, resourcefulness, bravery and persistence. Here, she gives us a taste of exactly what it was like.

I have been asked to give you some sketches of my pioneer life, and if you will excuse a simple story told in a simple way, I will try to give you a few of the experiences which came to us: first on the long journey from Missouri to New Mexico; second, on the trip from New Mexico to Arizona, and others during our life on the cattle ranch on the Gila River, twenty miles south of Clifton, Arizona.

In the spring off 1873, a party of sixteen persons, four women, seven men and five children, started from the central part of Missouri to find homes in the far west; all were hoping to better their fortunes, and a few, including myself, were seeking health; some kind neighbours advised my husband to put a spade in the wagon thinking it might be needed, but I was anxious to make the trial.

Our train consisted of covered wagons, drawn by oxen and a herd of cattle, driven by the younger men who were on horses. Our long, tedious journey required four months. You will realise that our progress was slow because all our possessions such as food, clothing, bedding, cooking utensils and tents were packed in the wagons, besides the women and children. Nine miles a day was the average distance we covered. Travellers now going over the same route at an average of fifty miles an hour will, no doubt, think of us with pity – but though slow we were sure. We were fortunate in regard to the weather as there was not much rain. On stormy nights the men did the cooking while the women and children remained in the wagons or tents, but we were usually so cramped from sitting all day we were glad to get out for exercise, if possible. After we reached the plains, wood for cooking was our greatest problem and it was some time before the women would consent to use a fire made of buffalo chips. Afterwards we made a joke of it, and would laugh to see some of the fastidious young men come into camp with a sack of chips on their shoulders; the old chips that had laid there for years through all kinds of weather certainly made a wonderful fire. By that time another party of four men, driving a larger bunch of cattle, had joined us and we welcomed the addition, believing there was more safety in numbers. We could hear the prairie chickens most every morning and passed large herds of buffaloes at different times and saw many antelopes. Our men killed several antelopes and two buffaloes on the way and the fresh meat was very acceptable; however, I would not care for a diet of buffalo meat. One day they had wounded a large buffalo and chased it until it was very tired. Our camp happened to be in the way, so he came right through. The women and children took refuge in the wagons, much disturbed over the uninvited guest. The work that has been done to preserve the buffaloes reminds me of what I saw when we touched at one point in Western Kansas ... sportsmen on board the trains had shot the buffaloes down until they lay by the hundreds, and were left to decay without even removing the skins. It was pitiful to see an act of such vandalism.

When we came through the Sioux and Fox Indian Reservations in Western Kansas one of the men missed his dog. After we were camped he went back to look for it, but was unsuccessful, but when he became angry and drew his revolver the Indians took him into a tepee where the dog was tied; no doubt they were preparing to have a feast of dog meat.

The government had built good stone houses of two rooms for these Indians, but they would not use them and were living in ragged tepees nearby. They had used the floors and the window and door casings for fires.

We saw many Indians, but no hostiles, although we had been warned before starting not to cross the Arkansas River. I was fortunate in being the first to see the mountains, which to me was a glorious sight, as it was just at sunrise. None of the party had seen a mountain and all were very much excited with our first view of the Rockies in Colorado; we rejoiced, too, that we were nearing the promised land, and a land of promise it indeed proved to most of us. Some felt they were too far from civilisation and returned to the old home, but the families remained and prospered. It was a rough life, living in log cabins with dirt roofs, forty miles from a post office or supplies. An ox team was our only means of travel and yet we were gloriously full of life and health. We had lived at this beautiful place at the foot of the Rocky mountains three years when we learned that we were on the old Maxwell Grant and could get no title to the land. We had read of the possibilities of the Gila Valley, pronounced with a hard G, of course, so my husband decided to come still farther west and left us in the spring of 1877. In October of the same year he made arrangements with a Mr Chandler, who owned and operated a large ox train, to bring us a distance of five or six hundred miles; so with my two little daughters of eleven and six years and a baby girl fourteen months, we boarded an ox train, which consisted of sixteen immense wagons, each drawn by ten or twelve yoke of oxen. The one provided for us was a good-sized spring wagon with bows and canvas cover, trailed behind the last wagon. In this we carried our clothes and bedding; the bed was rolled up in the back of the wagon during the day; at night we spread it in the bottom and made a fairly comfortable bed. The man who owned the train promised to make the trip in six weeks, but on account of having poor oxen and en- countering stormy weather, we were almost three months on the way. Some nights the oxen would wander so far they could not be found in time to move on next day and we would be compelled to remain in camp much against our will, for when we were moving, even if it were ever so little, we felt we were drawing nearer the end of our journey. The drivers were all Mexicans. After camp was made at night and the teams were turned loose a large fire was built for the men, and a smaller was made near our wagon. The provisions and cooking utensils were brought to my wagon as, unless it was very cold or snowing, I did my own cooking. In case of stormy weather food was brought to us. If there was snow the men would scrape it off, cut pine boughs and build a wind break, then we would wrap up and sit out by the fire. They were good to the children and would want to hold them. This would have been a rest for me, as I had to hold my baby all day to keep her from falling out of the wagon, but they were so filthy and infested with vermin I didn't dare allow them to help me, and as it was we did not entirely escape. We learned a few Mexican words, the alphabet and how to count. Mr Chandler said we were not to ask the meaning of their songs as we could enjoy them better not to know. Since we were so long on the road our provisions gave out and we had to use the same food provided for the Mexicans; beans, flour, coffee, bacon and dried fruit. One night we camped near a white family who was going in the opposite direction; the man had killed a bear and gave us some of the meat, which we enjoyed. These were the only white people I saw after leaving Albuquerque and we passed through no towns except little Mexican plazas.

Mr Chandler had told us what route we would take and the towns we would pass through so I could get mail, but after he started he changed his route twice and I had not a line from anyone for almost three months. My people back in the old home, thinking we were at the mercy of half savages, as they judged the Mexicans to be, were very anxious, and my husband was anxious, too, although he had confidence in the man's promise to bring us through safely. Fortunately, we were perfectly well all the time. If any of us had been seriously ill nothing could have been done. One Mexican did die one night in the wagon next to ours. We heard him moaning and calling on God to help; it was bitterly cold and no one went to him. The next morning they seemed very much surprised to find him dead. We had to stay over one day so they could carry the body to a little plaza and lay it in consecrated ground. I thought it would have been more Christian to have taken care of him while he was alive.

The train moved so slowly we would take turns walking in good weather and could easily keep up with the wagons. The children gathered quantities of pinon nuts and in the evening the men helped to roast them.

We passed many hours cracking and eating them as we moved along.

The first word I had from my husband was a note sent by some teamsters. This message reached me fifty miles out of Silver City. Two days afterwards he met us with a light wagon and a team of large mules. That was a joyful meeting and we gladly said goodbye to the plodding old oxen. It seemed that we were flying as we bowled along the last twenty-five miles to Silver City, where we arrived at six o'clock in the evening to find our little adobe house all ready for us, even the wood was laid ready for a fire in the Mexican fireplace, built in one corner of the room. How good it was to feel a floor under our feet and to have a comfortable bed on which to rest! My husband was very proud to think I would undertake such a journey to be with him, but I told him to make the most of it for, knowing what it meant, I would never do it again, alone.

I have made other journeys equally as tiresome and dangerous, when one was afraid of Indians behind every tree or rock. If we were travelling by night we imagined every soap weed was an enemy running, but he was with us and told us never to look for an Indian, because he would always hear the shot first.

Silver City, where we arrived the last of December, 1877, was quite a small place then. It is the county seat of Grant County, New Mexico, and at that time the silver mines were in active operation. There were also many large and small cattle ranches and sheep herds scattered over the country and a number of small farms or ranches, as we call them in this western country. These were located in the valleys around and all were drawing their supplies from Silver City, which trading made the town a very flourishing and prosperous place. It is beautifully situated and has a fine climate. We remained in this place, where my husband was engineer in the smelter, for over two years, then he took a herd of cattle on shares from Harvey Whitehill, sheriff of the county, and moved them out on the Gila river only a few miles from the Arizona line. After the cattle were located he returned for the family and we again embarked in a wagon, but this time it was drawn by horses. We were only two days making the trip over the Continental Divide, through the Burro mountains by way of Knight's Ranch. There we saw the burned remains of a wagon, household goods and wearing apparel scattered about where the Indians had massacred a family a short time before. We passed over a long dry mesa to a crossing on the Gila and drove down the valley past a few scattered ranches to the cattle ranch where we were to live for a year in a Jacel house, made by setting posts close together in the ground and daubing them with mud. It had a dirt roof and floor. While we lived at this place I taught school in one of the rooms, having an enrolment of nine children, including my two. With the proceeds of this venture I bought my first sewing machine. After a year we moved fourteen miles down the river into Arizona and settled on government land, which is now called York Flat. There were a few shacks on the place, and my husband soon had built a large adobe house with shingle roof, windows and floors which were a real luxury. Here we felt at home once more. Our house was a stopping place for travellers going from the railroad at Lordsburg to Clifton and the Longfellow Mines, which were owned and controlled by the Lesinskys. We entertained a number of interesting people; men who would be welcome guests in any society and more than welcome to us. They were very cordial and friendly and made an effort to give us the news of the outside world.

Some of those I like to remember were Colonel Lee and Governor Sheldon, of Santa Fe; H. W. Lawton, Gen. John A. Logan, the Churches, who were the first owners of the mines at Morenci; many army officers, and Archibald Clavering Gunter, a story writer, who wrote profusely. One of his most interesting stories is 'Miss Nobody of Nowhere', a rather exciting story of Indian troubles in the neighbourhood of the ranch. The Indians were hostile and made a raid somewhere through the country twice a year, in the spring and fall when the grass and water was plentiful for their ponies. One time all the settlers got together about twenty miles up the river, making the trip at night because the Indians never attack at night or during a storm. We stayed at that ranch a week; sometimes the men would fill gunny sacks with sand and pack the windows half way and we would stay at the ranch. At other times everyone forted at Duncan and on this occasion the cowboys followed the Indians several days and pressed them so closely a squaw dropped her papoose which was strapped in the basket. The baby was so filthy the women had trouble getting it clean. A family named Adams took the child, a boy, and as he grew he developed the Indian traits. He was very cruel with other children and often struck at them with a hammer or rock. At one time he slashed a little boy with a knife, but was caught before the boy was badly hurt. The Indians travelled fast, only stopping long enough to run off the horses or kill a beef or human being they found. I do not remember them ever attacking a house, for the Apache Indians are great cowards and never fight in the open. A rattlesnake is a more honest enemy, because he, at least, warns one before striking. At one time five hundred Indians passed the ranch and, as it was round-up time, they killed a good many cattle and one man in sight of the house and two others a few miles above. Another time we heard the shot that killed a young man who had been at the ranch an hour before, playing croquet. There are many other incidents I could mention, but will not at this time.

If the men were late coming in from their rides after the cattle I was very uneasy and could not rest. My husband would scoldingly say that he always trailed a cow until he found her, and that I must get used to his being away. I often told him the day might come when he would wish I would become uneasy and send men to hunt him. This proved true, for if I had known it was Indians instead of rustlers who had stolen our horses three years later I would have sent men to his relief and he would not have been ambushed and killed.

After my husband's death I was compelled to remain at the ranch, as all we had was there. With the five children, the oldest sixteen and the youngest eight months, I went through many rough and dangerous experiences. The children's education was a serious problem. I tried taking them to California, but things went wrong at the ranch and I was sent for. I brought with me a young lady teacher, who stayed with us two years and took entire charge of the children; then we had another teacher for the same length of time. Altogether we had four and this arrangement proved much more satisfactory than sending them away from home.

Many things crowd into my mind, but I shall bring my story to a close by saying to you dear young people, who are starting out in life and are feeling, sometimes, that you are having many hardships to contend with in these rough mining camps, that if you just stop and think how much better you are situated than we of the earlier days were, you will have very much to be appreciative and thankful for.

Anger in Saigon

from *All the Wrong Places:*
 Adrift in the Politics of Asia

by James Fenton

In 1973 James Fenton is in Saigon, a city in South Vietnam,
staying – as most British journalists did – in the Hotel Royale.
He is there to report on the Vietnam War (1964–75), in which
huge US military forces helped South Vietnam fight North
Vietnam. 'I had to find work. I had to sell some stories . . .' he
writes, but he feels infected by the epidemic of anxiety and
distress sweeping over them all. He finds himself especially
moved and angered by the suffering of the children.

Of all the ingenious and desperate forms of raising
money, the practice of drugging your baby and laying
the thing on the pavement in front of the visitor
seemed to me the most repulsive. It did not take long to
see that none of these children was ever awake during
the day, or to notice from the way they slept that something was amiss. Among the foreigners, stories circulated about the same baby being seen in the arms of five
different mothers in one week, but the beggar who
regularly sat outside the Royale always had the same
child, a girl of eighteen months or so. I never gave any
money either to the girl and her 'mother' or to any
other such teams.

One day, however, I was returning from a good lunch
when I saw that a crowd had formed around the old
woman, who was wailing and gesticulating. The child
was more than usually grey, and there were traces of
vomit around her face. People were turning her over,

slapping her, trying to force her eyes open. At one point she and the old woman were bundled into a taxi. Then they were taken out again and the slapping was repeated. I went into the hotel and told the girl at reception to call a doctor. 'No,' she replied. 'But the child is sick.' 'If baby go to hospital or doctor' – and here she imitated an injection – 'then baby die.''No,' I replied, 'if baby *don't* go to hospital maybe baby die.' 'No.'

I took the girl out into the street, where the scene had taken on the most grotesque appearance. All the beggars I had ever seen in Saigon seemed to have gathered, and from their filthy garments they were producing pins and sticking them under the child's toenails. 'You see,' I said to the girl, 'no good, number ten. Baby need number-one hospital.' 'No, my grandmother had same thing. She need this – number one.' And the receptionist produced a small phial of eucalyptus oil. 'That's not number one,' I said, 'that's number ten. Number ten thousand,' I added for emphasis. But it was no good insisting or appealing to other members of the crowd. Everybody was adamant that if the child was taken to the hospital, the doctor would kill it with an injection. While I correspondingly became convinced that a moment's delay would cost the child's life.

Finally, after a long eucalyptus massage and repeated pricking of the fingers and toes had produced no visible results, I seemed to win. If I would pay for taxi and hospital, the woman would come. I pushed my way through the crowd and dragged her towards the taxi – a battered old Renault tied together with string. The baby was wrapped in a tarpaulin and her face covered with a red handkerchief. Every time I tried to remove the handkerchief, from which came the most ominous dry gaspings, the woman replaced it. I directed the taxi-driver to take us to number-one hospital and we set off. But from the start everything went wrong. Within a hundred yards we had to stop for gas. Then a van stalled in front of us, trapping the taxi. Next, to my amazement, we came to what must have been, I thought, the only level-crossing in Saigon, where as it happened a train was expected in the near future. And around here we were hit by the side effects of Typhoon Sarah, which at the time was causing havoc in the northern provinces. We also split a tyre, though this was not noticed till later. Driving on through the cloudburst, the taxi driver seemed strangely unwilling to hurry. So I sat in the back seat keeping one hand on the horn and the other attempting to alleviate the restrictions around the baby's breathing apparatus. I also recall producing a third arm with which to comfort the old woman from time to time and I remember that her shoulder, when my hand rested on it, was very small and very hard. Everything, I said, was going to be number one, okay: number-one hospital, number-one doctor, babysan okay. We were travelling through Cholon, the Chinese quarter, on an errand of Western mercy.

All things considered, it took a long time for it to dawn on me that we were not going to a hospital at all. We even passed a first-aid post without the driver giving it a glance. In my mind there was an image of the sort of thing required: a large cool building dating from French times, recently refurbished by American aid and charity, with some of the best equipment in the East. I could even imagine the sententious plaques on the walls. Perhaps there would be a ward named after the former U.S. ambassador. It would be called the Bunker Ward.

It was when the old woman began giving directions

that I saw I had been duped. We were now threading our way through some modern slums, which looked like the Chinese equivalent of the Isle of Dogs. 'Where is the hospital? This is no hospital,' I said. Yes, yes, the taxi-driver replied, we were going to hospital, number-one doctor. We stopped by a row of shops and the driver got out. I jumped from the car and seized him by the arm, shouting: 'I said number-one hospital. You lie. You cheap charlie. You number-ten-thousand Saigon.' We were surrounded by children, in the pouring rain, the taxi man tugging himself free, and me gripping him by the arm. It was left to the woman, carrying the little bundle of tarpaulin, to find out exactly where the doctor lived. Finally I gave in, and followed her up some steps, then along an open corridor lined with tailors and merchants. At least, I thought, when the baby dies I can't be blamed. And once I had thought that, the thought turned into a wish: A little cough would have done it, a pathetic gurgle, then a silence, and my point about Western medicine would have been proved to my own satisfaction. I should have behaved very well; of course I should have paid for, and gone to, the funeral.

In retrospect it was easy to see how the establishment would command confidence: the dark main room with its traditional furnishings, the walls lined with photographs of ancestors in traditional Vietnamese robes, a framed jigsaw of the Italian lakes. And in the back room (it would, of course, have to be a back room) a plump, middle-aged lady was massaging the back of another plump, middle-aged lady. They paid hardly any attention when we came in. There was not the slightest element of drama. Indeed, I began to see that I was now the only person who was panicking. When she had finished the massage, the doctor turned her attention to the baby. First she took some ointment from a dirty bowl at her elbow, and rubbed it all over the little grey body. Then from another bowl she produced some pink substance resembling Euthymol toothpaste, with which she proceeded to line the mouth. In a matter of minutes, the child was slightly sick, began to cry, and recovered. I had never been more furious in my life. To complete my humiliation, the doctor refused any payment. She provided the old woman with a prescription wrapped in newspaper, and we left. We drove to the miserable shelter in which the old woman lived. 'Sit down,' she said, indicating the wooden bed which was the only feature of her home apart from the roof (there were no walls). In any other mood I might have been moved by the fact that the only English she knew beyond the terrible pidgin currency of the beggars was a phrase of hospitality. But I so deeply hated her at that moment that I could only give her a couple of pounds, plus some useless advice about keeping the baby warm and off the pavements, and go.

I left the taxi-driver at a garage not far from the Royale, where I also gave him some money toward repairing the split tyre. 'You number one, Saigon,' he said, with a slight note of terror in his voice. The weather had cleared up, and I strolled along past the market stalls. You could buy U.S. Army foot-powder in bulk, K-rations, lurp rations (for Long Range Reconnaissance Patrols), souvenir Zippo lighters (engraved 'Yea though I walk through the valley of the shadow of death I shall fear no evil, for I am the evilest sonofabitch in the valley'), khaki toothbrushes and flannels, and model helicopters constructed out of used hypodermics. You could also buy jackets brightly embroidered with the words 'When I die I shall go to heaven, for I have spent my time in hell – Saigon,' and a collection of GI cartoons and jokes called *Sorry 'bout that, Vietnam.* As I approached the hotel, people began asking how the baby was, and smiling when I replied 'Okay.'

And I began to think, supposing they were all in it together? Suppose the old woman, the taxi driver, the man whose van stalled, the engine driver – suppose they were all now dividing out the proceeds and having a good laugh at my expense, congratulating the child on the way it had played its role? That evening I would be telling the story to some old Saigon hand when a strange pitying smile would come over his face. 'You went to Cholon did you? Describe the doctor...uhuh... Was there a jigsaw puzzle of the Italian lakes? Well, well, well. So they even used the toothpaste trick. Funny how the oldest gags are still the best....'

Indeed I did have rather that conversation a few days later, with an American girl, a weaver. It began 'You realise, of course, first of all that the taxi driver was the husband of the old woman ... But I do not think it was a conspiracy.' Worse, I should rather conclude that the principals involved were quite right not to trust the hospital doctors with a beggar's child. It was for this reason that the hotel receptionist had countermanded my orders to the taxi man, I learned afterwards, and many people agreed with her.

When the old woman came on the streets, I hardly recognised either her or the child, who for the first time looked conscious and well. 'Babysan okay now, no sick,' she said, gazing at me with an awful adoring expression, though the hand was not stretched out for money. And when I didn't reply she turned to the child and told it something in the same unctuous tones. This performance went on for the rest of my stay: Whenever

I was around, the child would be made to look at the kind foreigner who had saved its life. I had indeed wanted to save the child's life, but not in *that* way, not on the old woman's terms.

I was disgusted, not just at what I saw around me, but at what I saw in myself. I saw how perilously thin was the line between the charitable and the murderous impulse, how strong the force of righteous indignation. I could well imagine that most of those who came to Vietnam to fight were not the evilest sons-of-bitches in the valley. It was just that, beyond the bright circle illuminated by their intelligence, in which everything was under their control and every person a compliant object, they came across a second person – a being or a nation with a will of its own, with its own medicine, whether Fishing Pills or pink toothpaste, and its own ideas for the future. And in the ensuing encounter everything had turned to justifiable ashes. It was impossible in Saigon to be the passive observer. Saigon cast you, inevitably, into the role of the American.

On the Way to Pretoria

from *An Autobiography: The Story of
My Experiments with Truth*

by Mohandas Gandhi

Gandhi, the great Indian political leader, went to South Africa
in 1893 to work as a lawyer. He has been asked to travel to
Pretoria from Durban to take part in a lawsuit there. Far from
his home in India, he is deeply troubled by the racism he
encounters. Indians are meant to travel in the third-class
compartments, but, characteristically, Gandhi quietly
determines to travel as he can afford to – in the first class.

On the seventh or eighth day after my arrival, I left
Durban. A first-class seat was booked for me. It was
usual there to pay five shillings extra, if one needed a
bedding. Abdulla Sheth insisted that I should book one
bedding but, out of obstinacy and pride and with a view
to saving five shillings, I declined. Abdulla Sheth
warned me. 'Look, now,' said he, 'this is a different
country from India. Thank God, we have enough and
to spare. Please do not stint yourself in anything that
you may need.'

I thanked him and asked him not to be anxious.

The train reached Maritzburg, the capital of Natal, at
about 9 p.m. Beddings used to be provided at this
station. A railway servant came and asked me if I
wanted one. 'No,' said I, 'I have one with me.' He went
away. But a passenger came next, and looked me up
and down. He saw that I was a 'coloured' man. This
disturbed him. Out he went and came in again with one
or two officials. They all kept quiet, when another

official came to me and said, 'Come along, you must go to the van compartment.'

'But I have a first-class ticket,' said I.

'That doesn't matter,' rejoined the other. 'I tell you, you must go to the van compartment.'

'I tell you, I was permitted to travel in this compartment at Durban, and I insist on going on in it.'

'No, you won't,' said the official. 'You must leave this compartment, or else I shall have to call a police constable to push you out.'

'Yes, you may. I refuse to get out voluntarily.'

The constable came. He took me by the hand and pushed me out. My luggage was also taken out. I refused to go to the other compartment and the train steamed away. I went and sat in the waiting room, keeping my hand-bag with me, and leaving the other luggage where it was. The railway authorities had taken charge of it.

It was winter, and winter in the higher regions of South Africa is severely cold. Maritzburg being at a high altitude, the cold was extremely bitter. My overcoat was in my luggage, but I did not dare to ask for it lest I should be insulted again, so I sat and shivered. There was no light in the room. A passenger came in at about midnight and possibly wanted to talk to me. But I was in no mood to talk.

I began to think of my duty. Should I fight for my rights or go back to India, or should I go on to Pretoria without minding the insults, and return to India after finishing the case? It would be cowardice to run back to India without fulfilling my obligation. The hardship to which I was subjected was superficial – only a symptom of the deep disease of colour prejudice. I should try, if possible, to root out the disease and suffer hardships in the process. Redress for wrongs I should seek only to the extent that would be necessary for the removal of the colour prejudice.

So I decided to take the next available train to Pretoria.

The following morning I sent a long telegram to the General Manager of the Railway and also informed Abdulla Sheth, who immediately met the General Manager. The Manager justified the conduct of the railway authorities, but informed him that he had already instructed the Station Master to see that I reached my destination safely. Abdulla Sheth wired to the Indian merchants in Maritzburg and to friends in other places to meet me and look after me. The merchants came to see me at the station and tried to comfort me by narrating their own hardships and explaining that what had happened to me was nothing unusual. They also said that Indians travelling first or second class had to expect trouble from railway officials and white passengers. The day was thus spent in listening to these tales of woe. The evening train arrived. There was a reserved berth for me. I now purchased at Maritzburg the bedding ticket I had refused to book at Durban.

The train took me to Charlestown.

The train reached Charlestown in the morning. There was no railway, in those days, between Charlestown and Johannesburg, but only a stage-coach, which halted at Standerton for the night *en route*. I possessed a ticket for the coach, which was not cancelled by the break of the journey at Maritzburg for a day; besides, Abdulla Sheth had sent a wire to the coach agent at Charlestown.

But the agent only needed a pretext for putting me off, and so, when he discovered me to be a stranger, he said, 'Your ticket is cancelled.' I gave him the proper reply. The reason at the back of his mind was not want of accommodation, but quite another. Passengers had to be accommodated inside the coach, but as I was regarded as a 'coolie' and looked a stranger, it would be proper, thought the 'leader', as the white man in charge of the coach was called, not to seat me with the white passengers. There were seats on either side of the coachbox. The leader sat on one of these as a rule. Today he sat inside and gave me his seat. I knew it was sheer injustice and an insult, but I thought it better to pocket it. I could not have forced myself inside, and if I had raised a protest, the coach would have gone off without me. This would have meant the loss of another day, and Heaven only knows what would have happened the next day. So, much as I fretted within myself, I prudently sat next the coachman.

At about three o'clock the coach reached Pardekoph. Now the leader desired to sit where I was seated, as he wanted to smoke and possibly to have some fresh air. So he took a piece of dirty sackcloth from the driver, spread it on the footboard and, addressing me, said, '*Sami*, you sit on this, I want to sit near the driver.' The insult was more than I could bear. In fear and trembling I said to him, 'It was you who seated me here, though I should have been accommodated inside. I put up with the insult. Now that you want to sit outside and smoke, you would have me sit at your feet. I will not do so, but I am prepared to sit inside.'

As I was struggling through these sentences, the man came down upon me and began heavily to box my ears. He seized me by the arm and tried to drag me down. I clung to the brass rails of the coachbox and was determined to keep my hold even at the risk of breaking my wristbones. The passengers were witnessing the scene – the man swearing at me, dragging and belabouring me, and I remaining still. He was strong and I was weak. Some of the passengers were moved to pity and exclaimed: 'Man, let him alone. Don't beat him. He is not to blame. He is right. If he can't stay there, let him come and sit with us.' 'No fear,' cried the man, but he seemed somewhat crestfallen and stopped beating me. He let go my arm, swore at me a little more, and asking the Hottentot servant who was sitting on the other side of the coachbox to sit on the footboard, took the seat so vacated.

The passengers took their seats and, the whistle given, the coach rattled away. My heart was beating fast within my breast, and I was wondering whether I should ever reach my destination alive. The man cast an angry look at me now and then and, pointing his finger at me, growled: 'Take care, let me once get to Standerton and I shall show you what I do.' I sat speechless and prayed to God to help me.

After dark we reached Standerton and I heaved a sigh of relief on seeing some Indian faces. As soon as I got down, these friends said: 'We are here to receive you and take you to Isa Sheth's shop. We have had a telegram from Dada Abdulla.' I was very glad, and we went to Sheth Isa Haji Summar's shop. The Sheth and his clerks gathered round me. I told them all that I had gone through. They were very sorry to hear it and comforted me by relating to me their own bitter experiences.

I wanted to inform the agent of the Coach Company of the whole affair. So I wrote him a letter, narrating everything that had happened, and drawing his attention to the threat his man had held out. I also asked for an assurance that he would accommodate me with the other passengers inside the coach when we started the next morning. To which the agent replied to this effect:

'From Standerton we have a bigger coach with different men in charge. The man complained of will not be there tomorrow, and you will have a seat with the other passengers.' This somewhat relieved me. I had, of course, no intention of proceeding against the man who had assaulted me, and so the chapter of the assault closed there.

In the morning Isa Sheth's man took me to the coach, I got a good seat and reached Johannesburg quite safely that night.

Standerton is a small village and Johannesburg a big city. Abdulla Sheth had wired to Johannesburg also, and given me the name and address of Muhammad Kasam Kamruddin's firm there. Their man had come to receive me at the stage, but neither did I see him nor did he recognise me. So I decided to go to a hotel. I knew the names of several. Taking a cab I asked to be driven to the Grand National Hotel. I saw the Manager and asked for a room. He eyed me for a moment, and politely saying, 'I am very sorry, we are full up', bade me goodbye. So I asked the cabman to drive to Muhammad Kasam Kamruddin's shop. Here I found Abdul Gani Sheth expecting me, and he gave me a cordial greeting. He had a hearty laugh over the story of my experience at the hotel. 'How ever did you expect to be admitted to a hotel?' he said.

'Why not?' I asked.

'You will come to know after you have stayed here a few days,' said he. 'Only *we* can live in a land like this, because, for making money, we do not mind pocketing insults, and here we are.' With this he narrated to me the story of the hardships of Indians in South Africa. ...

He said: 'This country is not for men like you. Look now, you have to go to Pretoria tomorrow. You will *have* to travel third class. Conditions in the Transvaal are worse than in Natal. First- and second-class tickets are never issued to Indians.'

'You cannot have made persistent efforts in this direction.'

'We have sent representations, but I confess our own men too do not want as a rule to travel first or second.'

I sent for the railway regulations and read them. There was a loophole. The language of the old Transvaal enactments was not very exact or precise; that of the railway regulations was even less so.

I said to the Sheth: 'I wish to go first class, and if I cannot, I shall prefer to take a cab to Pretoria, a matter of only thirty-seven miles.'

Sheth Abdul Gani drew my attention to the extra time and money this would mean, but agreed to my proposal to travel first, and accordingly we sent a note to the Station Master. I mentioned in my note that I was a barrister and that I always travelled first. I also stated in the letter that I needed to reach Pretoria as early as possible, that as there was no time to await his reply I would receive it in person at the station, and that I should expect to get a first-class ticket. There was of course a purpose behind asking for the reply in person. I thought that, if the Station Master gave a written reply, he would certainly say 'no', especially because he would have his own notion of a 'coolie' barrister. I would therefore appear before him in faultless English dress, talk to him and possibly persuade him to issue a first-class ticket. So I went to the station in a frock-coat and necktie, placed a sovereign for my fare on the counter and asked for a first-class ticket.

'You sent me that note?' he asked.

'That is so. I shall be much obliged if you will give me a ticket. I must reach Pretoria today.'

He smiled, and moved to pity, said: 'I am not a Transvaaler. I am a Hollander. I appreciate your feelings, and you have my sympathy. I do want to give you a ticket – on one condition, however, that, if the guard should ask you to shift to the third class, you will not involve me in the affair, by which I mean that you should not proceed against the Railway Company. I wish you a safe journey. I can see you are a gentleman.'

With these words he booked the ticket. I thanked him and gave him the necessary assurance.

Sheth Abdul Gani had come to see me off at the station. The incident gave him an agreeable surprise, but he warned me saying: 'I shall be thankful if you reach Pretoria all right. I am afraid the guard will not leave you in peace in the first class, and even if he does, the passengers will not.'

I took my seat in a first-class compartment and the train started. At Germiston the guard came to examine the tickets. He was angry to find me there, and signalled to me with his finger to go to the third class. I showed him my first-class ticket. 'That doesn't matter,' said he, 'remove to the third class.'

There was only one English passenger in the compartment. He took the guard to task. 'What do you mean by troubling the gentleman?' he said. 'Don't you see he has a first-class ticket? I do not mind in the least his travelling with me.' Addressing me, he said, 'You should make yourself comfortable where you are.'

The guard muttered: 'If you want to travel with a coolie, what do I care?' and went away.

At about 8 o'clock in the evening the train reached Pretoria.

The Crocodile's Bite

from *The Sepik and the Waghi*

by Christina Dodwell

Christina Dodwell is an experienced traveller and wants to return to one special place in New Guinea.

There was one other special village that I wanted to revisit, Kraimbit, where I had stayed for a month in 1980. Kraimbit lies far up the Blackwater tributary river so I borrowed a motor-canoe for two days. The journey to Kraimbit wasn't easy because, this being the dry season, the water-level was 15 to 20 feet lower than on my previous visit, and what had formerly been a maze of lakes and rivers was now a vast mud-flat with a few streams. The canoe kept running aground and the boatman said he was lost. Finally I got out to see if I could find out where we were, but after a short distance I walked into deep mud, suddenly sinking to my hips in wet ooze which cloyed around my legs. I had to struggle quite hard to get back on to firm ground. After floundering out, hot, wet and mud-covered, I went and lay in the stream to wash the mud off before rejoining the boatman. But I refused to feel ruffled, telling myself that one must not expect things to be easy; after all, this is New Guinea. And I was looking forward to reaching Kraimbit again, having kept in touch with people there over several years by letter (airmail/canoemail). Finally some children in a paddle-canoe came along and, promising to send help back to the boatman, I took a lift with the children to Kraimbit.

When the Kraimbits saw me arrive they began calling to each other in excitement and many came running through the village. It was a wonderful welcome; I shook hands with everyone and couldn't stop smiling while their eyes shone and their faces beamed with pleasure. Some *bigmen* and the headman, Kansol Otto, hurried over to welcome me. They took me to a shade-shelter, brought fruit for refreshment, and we all sat down together to exchange news.

One major event for them had been the construction of a new *haus tamboran*, a magnificent, large house on carved stilts which dominated the centre of the village. Traditional, spiritual beliefs are rigorously followed here; Kansol Otto had not allowed me to use the men's path, but had brought me on the women's path, and I wondered if I would be admitted into this new *haus tamboran*. I had been the only woman to go into their last one; at the time they had said that because of the way I had come to visit them – alone, by canoe – they would give me the freedom of the *haus tamboran* and treat me as an honorary man.

So I asked Otto if the committee of the *haus tamboran* would let me inside this new one. Otto's face clouded over and he fumbled for words. The hesitation surprised me, but soon I realised that it came from their fear of the *tamboran* and its power; they didn't want to put me in danger.

After a meeting of elders it was decided that I should be reinitiated into the new *haus tamboran*, along with some other initiates. I was guided to a line of solemn men which I joined and we walked along the men's path and up the bamboo ladder into the *haus*. In the shady half-light I presented gifts to the committee, Otto and various *bigmen*, under the eye of the *tamboran*. Five old men began playing their sacred bamboo 'flutes';

holding the long, fat bamboo tubes out sideways, they danced in circles, all keeping the same complex foot-rhythm, and blowing through the bamboo to produce mellow, braying harmonies. Some bamboo flutes were decorated with canework and feathers, some can only be played by one man and are thought to have the power to produce only one specific song.

Otto brought my attention to a group of boys and young men, and said that they were now ready for their initiation into manhood through the skin-cutting ordeal. This is a blood ritual dedicated to crocodiles, a rare and dramatic ceremony at which the initiates' bodies are cut and sliced to represent their battle with the Devil crocodile, and their rebirth as crocodile-men.

If I look at this from a westerner's viewpoint it seems a barbaric and savage ritual, but from the Kraimbits' perspective it is the customary mark of manhood and they bear the scars with pride. The initiates explained to me that by going voluntarily through the pain and fear of the ceremony they would emerge as men, wearing the scars as an outward sign of their courage and fortitude, and as a reminder that they should never again be afraid. One initiate, Rassell, was only twelve years old and he was clearly terrified of the whole idea, but he said that he was ready to face it. Many of the men sitting around me had the scars of skin-cutting; raised series of bumps from their backs over their shoulders and down to their stomachs, with crocodile eyes cut on their chests.

Everything was ready, people were in a festive mood, and after a while the committee announced that the initiation would start that evening.

In the late afternoon the villagers went to decorate themselves, painting coloured mud ochres on their bodies and shaking out their head-dresses of fur and feathers. I went to wash at a small, cool spring in the sago-palm forest, using a coconut-shell to scoop up the water and pour it over myself. Then I hurried back to watch the menfolk, now in full *bilas* (body decoration), marching through the village and into the *haus tamboran*. Soon the throbbing of drums began to resound from the *haus*.

The women were chanting and dancing around outside the *haus*, dancing with small steps and flicking their hips to swing their grass skirts. At dusk the initiates were brought outside like prisoners with their hands held above their heads and grasses in their mouths. Suddenly the women surged forward and pretended to try to wrestle their sons from the men's grasp, but after a scuffle they were beaten into retreat, and the boys went back inside the *haus*. Papa Lucas (my proxy father in Kraimbit) took me with them up the ladder into the *haus*, into a scene of drumming and dancing as men stomped in rings, jangling their shell leg-bands and chanting in rising waves of oh-ee-ay.

As more men gradually joined in the dance they formed wheels within wheels, each going at a different speed. They kept it up all night, while the women held a different kind of *singsing* in a big family house nearby. Long after dark when I left the *haus tamboran* and went to the women's house, I found the women sitting cross-legged on the floor around some kerosene lanterns, mothering their babies and chanting a chorus, while in the centre of the hut three women stood singing solos, calling to their sons (the initiates) not to be afraid of the crocodile's bite. Other women stood to lead different chants; Papa Lucas' wife led a chant of happiness at my return and everyone in the house stood up to join in.

In the deep of the night I went back to the *haus*

tamboran to watch as the wheeling circle of men generated the power of the *tamboran*. Initiation includes the boys' entry into the secrets of their ancestors and nature spirits, things beyond the comprehensible, whose powers are called up during the night in rituals which are taboo to outsiders; it would not be proper to describe them here.

At dawn the three initiates were taken by a silent crocodile-line of men to wash in the creek, and when they came back they sat on *limbum* mats outside the *haus tamboran*, ready for the skin-cutting to begin.

The first cuts of the razor blades on the boys' chests drew half-circles around their nipples, four half-circles over a quarter-inch deep. Blood ran from the slashes and, feeling dizzy, I sat down hurriedly. Two initiates beside me were gritting their teeth against the pain, but the third, young Rassell, was screaming loudly with terror. I felt sorry for him but his companions told him sternly, 'We must bleed, to let out our mother's blood so we become men.'

His screams did not stop and after making the minimum markings the *haus tamboran*'s committee let him go, which was a relief since no one intended the boy to suffer overmuch. Meanwhile, on the other two boys' shoulders and backs the skincutters were making a wide series of slashes like scale-markings, and helpers used wodges of grass to mop away the flows of blood.

About an hour later when their skin-cutting was over, the boys' cuts were anointed with plant oil and red mud (which effectively prevents infections).

Then it was my turn. I wanted to complete my initiation into the new *haus tamboran*, feeling that I was no longer an outsider to the Sepik customs or to the people who had adopted me, and so I let the villagers mark me with the crocodile's bite on my left shoulder.

It was painful, and as the razor blade kept ripping through my skin, I winced and clenched my hands. Papa Lucas told me I must be brave in order to emerge strong, like a crocodile, never to be afraid again.

The cutting went on for about fifteen minutes. My arm was bleeding profusely and I didn't watch the cuts because I didn't want to faint, but afterwards when they washed it I saw that it was a diamond-shaped mark with decorative fletchings. When it had been anointed with oil and ochre the men took me back into the *haus tamboran* for a small ceremony that gave me the highest honours they could bestow. It was similar to the British custom of giving the freedom of a city to someone; the villagers told me that through my initiation I had become an honorary member of the Sepik region, that in my future visits every door would be open to me and I would be free to enter the deeper mysteries of Sepik life.

The Hopi Snake Dance

from *Mornings in Mexico*

by D.H. Lawrence

The famous writer D.H. Lawrence watches a dance among a
crowd eager for thrills and excited by the nearness of danger.
This is Mexico, in the 1920s: snakes are going to curl around,
and snake-priests will brave their poison.

By afternoon of the next day the three thousand people
had massed in the little *plaza*, secured themselves places
on the roof and in the window-spaces, everywhere, till
the small pueblo seemed built of people instead of
stones. All sorts of people, hundreds and hundreds of
white women, all in breeches like half-men, hundreds
and hundreds of men who had been driving motor-
cars, then many Navajos, the women in their full, long
skirts and tight velvet bodices, the men rather lanky,
long-waisted, real nomads. In the hot sun and the wind
which blows the sand every day, every day in volumes
round the corners, the three thousand tourists sat for
hours, waiting for the show. The Indian policeman
cleared the central oblong, in front of the kiva. The
front rows of onlookers sat thick on the ground. And at
last, rather early, because of the masses awaiting them,
suddenly, silently, in the same rude haste, the antelope-
priests filed absorbedly in, and made the rounds over
the lid, as before. Today, the eight antelope-priests were
very grey. Their feet ashed pure grey, like suède soft
boots: and their lower jaw was pure suède grey, while
the rest of their face was blackish. With that pale-grey

116

jaw, they looked like corpse-faces with swathing-bands. And all their bodies ash-grey smeared, with smears of black, and a black cloth today at the loins.

They made their rounds, and took their silent position behind the lid, with backs to the green tuft: an unearthly grey row of men with little skin bags in their hands. They were the lords of shadow, the intermediate twilight, the place of after-life and before-life, where house the winds of change. Lords of the mysterious, fleeting power of change.

Suddenly, with abrupt silence, in paced the snake-priests, headed by the same heavy man with solid grey hair like iron. Today they were twelve men, from the old one, down to the slight, short-haired, erect boy of fourteen. Twelve men, two for each of the six worlds, or quarters: east, north, south, west, above, and below. And today they were in a queer ecstasy. Their faces were black, showing the whites of the eyes. And they wore small black loin-aprons. They were the hot living men of the darkness, lords of the earth's inner rays, the black sun of the earth's vital core, from which dart the speckled snakes, like beams.

Round they went, in rapid, uneven, silent absorption, the three rounds. Then in a row they faced the eight ash-grey men, across the lid. All kept their heads bowed towards earth, except the young boys.

Then, in the intense, secret, muttering chant the grey men began their leaning from right to left, shaking the hand, one-two, one-two, and bowing the body each time from right to left, left to right, above the lid in the ground, under which were the snakes. And their low, deep, mysterious voices spoke to the spirits under the earth, not to men above the earth.

But the crowd was on tenterhooks for the snakes, and could hardly wait for the mummery to cease. There was an atmosphere of inattention and impatience. But the chant and the swaying passed from the grey men to the black-faced men, and back again, several times.

This was finished. The formation of the lines broke up. There was a slight crowding to the centre, round the lid. The old antelope-priest (so called) was stooping. And before the crowd could realise anything else a young priest emerged, bowing reverently, with the neck of a pale, delicate rattlesnake held between his teeth, the little, naïve, bird-like head of the rattlesnake quite still, near the black cheek, and the long, pale, yellowish, spangled body of the snake dangling like some thick, beautiful cord. On passed the black-faced young priest, with the wondering snake dangling from his mouth, pacing in the original circle, while behind him, leaping almost on his shoulders, was the oldest heavy priest, dusting the young man's shoulders with the feather-prayer-sticks, in an intense, earnest anxiety of concentration such as I have only seen in the old Indian men during a religious dance.

Came another young black-faced man out of the confusion, with another snake dangling and writhing a little from his mouth, and an elder priest dusting him from behind with the feathers: and then another, and another: till it was all confusion, probably, of six, and then four young priests with snakes dangling from their mouths, going round, apparently, three times in the circle. At the end of the third round the young priest stooped and delicately laid his snake on the earth, waving him away, away, as it were, into the world. He must not wriggle back to the kiva bush.

And after wondering a moment, the pale, delicate snake steered away with a rattlesnake's beautiful movement, rippling and looping, with the small, sensitive head lifted like antennae, across the sand to the massed audience squatting solid on the ground around. Like soft, watery lightning went the wondering snake at the crowd. As he came nearer, the people began to shrink aside, half-mesmerised. But they betrayed no exaggerated fear. And as the little snake drew very near, up rushed one of the two black-faced young priests who held the snake-stick, poised a moment over the snake, in the prayer-concentration of reverence which is at the same time conquest, and snatched the pale, long creature delicately from the ground, waving him in a swoop over the heads of the seated crowd, then delicately smoothing down the length of the snake with his left hand, stroking and smoothing and soothing the long, pale, bird-like thing; and returning with it to the kiva, handed it to one of the grey-jawed antelope-priests.

Meanwhile, all the time, the other young priests were emerging with a snake dangling from their mouths. The boy had finished his rounds. He launched his rattlesnake on the ground, like a ship, and like a ship away it steered. In a moment, after it went one of those two black-faced priests who carried snake-sticks and were the snake-catchers. As it neared the crowd, very close, he caught it up and waved it dramatically, his eyes glaring strangely out of his black face. And in the interim that youngest boy had been given a long, handsome bull-snake, by the priest at the hole under the kiva boughs. The bull-snake is not poisonous. It is a constrictor. This one was six feet long, with a sumptuous pattern. It waved its pale belly, and pulled its neck out of the boy's mouth. With two hands he put it back. It pulled itself once more free. Again he got it back, and managed to hold it. And then as he went round in his looping circle, it coiled its handsome folds twice round his knee. He stooped, quietly, and as quietly as if he were untying his garter, he unloosed the folds. And all the time, an old priest was intently brushing the boy's thin straight shoulders with the feathers. And all the time, the snakes seemed strangely gentle, naïve, wondering and almost willing, almost in harmony with the man. Which of course was the sacred aim. While the boy's expression remained quite still and simple, as it were candid, in a candour where he and the snake should be in unison. The only dancers who showed signs of being wrought-up were the two young snake-catchers, and one of these, particularly, seemed in a state of actor-like uplift, rather ostentatious. But the old priests had that immersed, religious intentness which is like a spell, something from another world.

The young boy launched his bull-snake. It wanted to go back to the kiva. The snake-catcher drove it gently forward. Away it went, towards the crowd, and at the last minute was caught up into the air. Then this snake was handed to an old man sitting on the ground in the audience, in the front row. He was an old Hopi of the Snake clan.

Snake after snake had been carried round in the circles, dangling by the neck from the mouths of one young priest or another, and writhing and swaying slowly, with the small, delicate snake-head held as if wondering and listening. There had been some very large rattlesnakes, unusually large, two or three handsome bull-snakes, and some racers, whipsnakes. All had been launched, after their circuits in the mouth, all had been caught up by the young priests with the snake-sticks, one or two had been handed to old-snake clan men in the audience, who sat holding them in their arms as men hold a kitten. The most of the snakes, however, had been handed to the grey antelope-men who stood in the row with their backs to the kiva bush. Till some of these ash-smeared men held armfuls of snakes, hanging over their arms like wet washing. Some of the snakes twisted and knotted round one another, showing pale bellies.

Yet most of them hung very still and docile. Docile, almost sympathetic, so that one was struck only by their clean, slim length of snake nudity, their beauty, like soft, quiescent lightning. They were so clean, because they had been washed and anointed and lustrated by the priests, in the days they had been in the kiva.

At last all the snakes had been mouth-carried in the circuits, and had made their little outrunning excursion to the crowd, and had been handed back to the priests in the rear. And now the Indian policemen, Hopi and Navajo, began to clear away the crowd that sat on the ground, five or six rows deep, around the small *plaza*. The snakes were all going to be set free on the ground. We must clear away.

We recoiled to the farther end of the *plaza*. There, two Hopi women were scattering white corn-meal on the sandy ground. And thither came the two snake-catchers, almost at once, with their arms full of snakes. And before we who stood had realised it, the snakes were all writhing and squirming on the ground, in the white dust of meal, a couple of yards from our feet. Then immediately, before they could writhe clear of each other and steer away, they were gently, swiftly snatched up again, and with their arms full of snakes, the two young priests went running out of the *plaza*.

We followed slowly, wondering, towards the western, or north-western edge of the mesa. There the mesa dropped steeply, and a broad trail wound down to the vast hollow of desert brimmed up with strong evening light, up out of which jutted a perspective of sharp rock and further mesas and distant sharp mountains: the great, hollow, rock-wilderness space of that part of Arizona, submerged in light.

Away down the trail, small, dark, naked, rapid figures with arms held close, went the two young men, running swiftly down to the hollow level, and diminishing, running across the hollow towards more stark rocks of the other side. Two small, rapid, intent, dwindling little human figures. The tiny, dark sparks of men. Such specks of gods. . . .

Soon after the dance is over, the Navajo begin to ride down the Western trail, into the light. Their women, with velvet bodices and full, full skirts, silver and turquoise tinkling thick on their breasts, sit back on their horses and ride down the steep slope, looking wonderingly around from their pleasant, broad, nomadic, Mongolian faces. And the men, long, loose, thin, long-waisted, with tall hats on their brows and low-sunk silver belts on their hips, come down to water their horses at the spring. We say they look wild. But they have the remoteness of their religion, their animistic vision, in their eyes, they can't see as we see. And they cannot accept us. They stare at us as the coyotes stare at us: the gulf of mutual negation between us.

So in groups, in pairs, singly, they ride silently down into the lower strata of light, the aboriginal Americans riding into their shut-in reservations. While the white Americans hurry back to their motor-cars, and soon the air buzzes with starting engines, like the biggest of rattlesnakes buzzing.

Study activities

Lift-off!

1 'The greatest week since Creation,' said President Richard Nixon, on 21 July 1969, after the first landing on the moon by Neil Armstrong and Buzz Aldrin. From far away, Armstrong uttered those famous words: 'That's one small step for man, one giant leap for mankind.' On television screens all over the world, the astronauts had roared out of the Earth's atmosphere and stuck a flag on the moon. Children were woken up at night to see the first human footstep on the Sea of Tranquillity. Was this Science Fiction coming to life? What changes in human life might it make possible? Could it solve the world's problems?

a) Try to describe what this first moon-landing may have meant to someone of your own age in 1969, a newly termed 'member of the moon generation'.

b) Does it move you? How has space travel since then affected people's lives and expectations?

2 What do you think it may have meant to be the first British person in space? Imagine you are Helen Sharman speaking to a press conference. What do you say? Prepare a speech explaining its significance.

3 Helen Sharman describes, in a later chapter of her book, some of the details of everyday living on board the spacecraft. Any unattached object drifts away and has to be fastened down with velcro; it means that after you eat, crumbs hang in the air. Going to the lavatory meant holding yourself *very* firmly in place! Darkness lasts

40 minutes and occurs 16 times a day; she would wash her hair using a special damp cloth and use the window at 'night-time' as a mirror.

If you were given the opportunity to become a member of a space team, what would you say? How well do you think you would adapt to the rigorous physical training, the claustrophobic living conditions of the rocket, and the fears and dangers involved in being far from Earth? Write about yourself.

4 Bill Anders, another astronaut, said, 'We came all this way to explore the moon, and the most important thing is that we discovered the Earth.' Helen Sharman shared his 'discovery' on her voyage. 'Our planet is endlessly, hypnotically beautiful . . . we frequently crossed Western Europe and of course I could see the distinctive shape of Britain . . . Down there were people I knew and loved, my friends and family.' She adds, 'Once passing over the Australian continent I saw two roads, each of them hundreds of miles long and running across the desert straight as a die, then meeting at a crossroad.'

What part(s) of the world would it move and excite you to see from space, and why?

A Glimpse of the Future?

1 What are the worst aspects of the New York subway?

a) Imagine that you are a frequent user of the subway. Write down the aspects of travelling that worry you most.

b) If you were a member of the organisation that controls the subway, which problems do you think you might be able to address yourself, and which do you think the government should take on? Prepare a speech to give to a committee set up to investigate.

c) As a member of the government, what is your response?

d) Use your classroom as a forum for a public meeting in which different parties express their views. You could have main speakers and the rest of the class as members of the public listening and giving their own opinions.

2 Your advertising agency has been given the task of advertising the Transit Police as a good career for young adults.

a) Write an advertisement for local and national newspapers outlining the job and giving details of the qualifications you think are necessary for it.

b) Write a script for a scene on prime television time making the work of the Transit Police look exciting and worthwhile.

c) Write down the thoughts of a seasoned police officer watching the scene.

d) Would you want the job? Give reasons for your answer.

A Decision

1 At the ceremony, Lynn Pan begins to suspect that she has been 'the poorer for being further cut off from folk and faith'. Write about your own experience of being a part of or distanced from your culture.

2 She cleverly uses Ah Sam's words, 'Shall we go back?' – meaning return to the house – to introduce the moment of realisation that she wanted to go back to what might be her real home: China. Describe what has brought her to this point.

3 Her mother and father looked back at China in different ways. Describe their attitudes and feelings.

4 In another part of the book, we learn about the time when her mother, separated from the children on leaving China, waited for them to join her in an inn in Macao.

> It was seedy even then, with scabs of damp on the walls. But it had those long windows, and they faced the river. At those windows you could see the boats come in. She brought a chair, making a little distance between herself and the window so she might take in the entire harbour. There she sat . . . She kept her eyes open, even when the day darkened. How long was it before she spotted our boat? Five days? Ten? I do not know. The only detail I remember her recounting is of her burning a green mosquito-repelling coil in a saucer and laying it down at her feet. And I did not know . . . why that single memory should bring me close to tears.

The tearing apart of families has been a consequence of events in nations all over the world in recent history. Take one example that you know of and try to explain why the children are particularly affected by this tragedy.

The Summit

1 The introduction to the 1835 edition tells us that the scenes Wordsworth describes are 'felt in the blood, and felt along the heart'. The writer says that the first object of the book is to give us information, but, 'just as a mother may reveal a depth of feeling by the tone of voice in which she tells the barest fact about her child, so Wordsworth cannot divorce his information from that emotion with which he always views his subject'.

In pairs, select four or five sentences that convey fact with depth of feeling in ways that show how effective this combination could be.

2 Look at Wordsworth's famous poem *The Prelude* to see how he describes the Lake District in verse. The passage beginning: 'The sands of Westmoreland, the creeks and bays . . .' is very powerful. What other passages can you find?

3 Have you ever had an experience like the one Wordsworth describes in this extract, where the beauty of a place has been intensified by the weather or the time of day? Write about it.

Parents

1 What made Freya Stark's father love Dartmoor so much? What might he have written about it in letters to his bride before she came? See if you can sum up his feelings, conveying their strength to her in a letter. Afterwards, write her reply. (Will you make her eager or apprehensive?)

2 Is there a place that means this much to you? (Or to someone you know?) Either write about it, or prepare to talk about it to others in the class. Include pictures if it helps.

3 Freya Stark's mother was effectively 'in exile' from her own country and from what she knew and loved. So are many others today. Movement, forced and voluntary, of peoples across countries and continents, is one of the great themes of our times.

Discuss with a partner what it might mean to be in exile, and then write a factual or imaginative account of someone who has suffered in this way.

Copenhagen

1 Bill Bryson is good at describing Copenhagen as a city for young people. What do you think young people might feel about the place you live in when they come to visit? Try to imagine it from their point of view and write a letter home from someone your own age describing her or his experiences.

2 Bryson is well known for his sense of humour. There are obvious dangers in being funny about countries other than your own. How well do you think he treads that fine line? Look at the extract again to see if there is anything that might offend anyone. Then try writing a humorous piece about your own country, avoiding, if you can, the pitfalls of stereotyping people and their behaviour. Test your skills by showing it to someone else in the class.

The Rapids of the Ogowé

1 European traders and Africans affectionately and respectfully called Mary Kingsley 'our own only me' after her usual method of introducing herself as she emerged 'unheralded out of the Bush in a dilapidated state'. It is said of her that her attitude to life could be summed up in the words of the nineteenth-century novelist George Eliot: 'God is conceivable, immortality is unbelievable, but duty is peremptory and absolute.'

What picture of Mary Kingsley are you able to form after reading the extract? Write a description of her. If you like, you could write it as if you knew her personally.

2 When she returned to England after an earlier journey in 1893, the press greeted her with a flourish. 'I discovered, to my alarm, that I was a freak of Fate, the sea-serpent of the season.' She didn't want to be seen as the dauntless lady-traveller, she wanted to be acknowledged for the priceless research she had done with plants, animals and insects.

Write two newspaper accounts of her return after her latest journey: one by a reporter who sees her as a woman first, and the second by a reporter who is excited by her finds.

3 Mary Kingsley was not only clever, brave and resourceful, she also had a strong sense of humour. Find some examples of this in the extract and discuss, in writing or by talking in groups, how they add to the flavour of her experiences and her writing.

Resisting Temptation

1 What do you think Iversen's thoughts were when he first dropped behind? Write them down.

2 Mikkelsen and Iversen had to walk on, keeping faith with themselves and each other. Do you think they believed that each would resist the temptation to turn the gun on the other? Write down their thoughts as they continued.

3 There are many other accounts of hunger that you can read about in travel writing; hunger is a risk you take when you set off on such expeditions. Nigel Ryan in *A Hitch or Two in Afghanistan* (Weidenfeld, 1983) describes the naked aggression between friends when both are hungry; he writes, 'For a pinprick in time the beast was let loose, then caged and barred again.' He adds, 'When survival is at risk survival is all that comes into the mind: honour and shame come a poor second. Perhaps hope brings out the worst in us all, including a mean streak in the will to survive; and it is only when hope has gone that there is room for the noble deeds that distinguish men from animals.' He then goes on to wonder about Captain Oates, who in 1912 went out of the tent to die on Scott's expedition to the Antarctic so that the others might stand a greater chance of survival, and about Mr Astor who gave up his place in a lifeboat when the *Titanic* was going down.

Write a short play in which a member of a group faces the conflict of personal sacrifice or survival.

The *Titanic*

1 Look at the figures following this account. What do they tell you about Britain's class system and how it affected chances of survival on board ship?

2 We know that the band continued playing until the very end. Suddenly no sound could be heard in the lifeboats except the music which wafted over the sea. It was a hymn . . .

> God of mercy and compassion
> Look with pity on my pain;
> Hear a mournful, broken spirit
> Prostrate at thy feet complain . . .
> Hold me up in mighty waters,
> Keep my eyes on things above.
> Righteousness, divine atonement,
> Peace and everlasting love.

While this was happening, many people were still floundering in the water and most were drowning. Afterwards, Third Officer Herbert J. Pitman was questioned by Senator Smith at the Inquiry as to why he, safe in a boat, did not return to those helpless people and pull them into the safety of the boats too. 'And you lay in the vicinity of that scene for about an hour?' the Senator asked. The Officer broke with emotion: 'Oh please, Sir, don't! I cannot bear to recall it.'

Describe the mingled terror and relief of someone in the boats as if it were an eye-witness account. You could do this in the form of a testimony at the Inquiry, or as an elderly man or woman telling his or her family about this many years later.

3 Feminists in America afterwards agreed that the policy of 'women and children first' in the lifeboats was unfair. If you wanted full equality with men, you should take equal risks too. A St Louis newspaper printed these verses:

> Votes for Women!
>   Was the cry
> Reaching upwards
>   To the sky
>
> Boats for Women!
>   Was the cry
> When the brave
>   Were come to die

What do *you* think? Discuss this in small groups.

Beyond the Golden Road

1 Michelle MacGrath describes her travels through
Uzbeki-stan, noting what she found to be exciting,
beautiful and different. Describe a time when you went
somewhere which you felt was compellingly different. It
doesn't have to be another country; sometimes another
part of your own country can seem very strange.
Sometimes just walking streets away from your usual
haunts can feel like this.

2 The written language of the Uzbeks is very poetic and has
changed alphabets three times in its history: Arabic letters
were used from the eighth century, then Roman letters,
and in 1940 the Russian alphabet was used. Other
important things changed too. The Russian Empire was
renamed the USSR (the Union of Soviet Socialist Republics)
after the Communist Revolution in 1917, and it compelled
different cultures with their independent languages to
submit to dictatorship from Moscow. Thus Uzbekistan
became part of Soviet Asia. In 1991, after the fall of
Communism, it was able to regain its freedom.

Uzbekistan is not the only State to undergo such changes.
Your school or local libraries may have an up-to-date atlas
which shows modern names of countries and the shape of
their boundaries. They will also almost certainly have older
ones that mark those places by their old names and shapes.
Really old atlases, pre-1939, for example, or earlier, will tell
an even more intriguing story about how the world looked.
See what you can find out.

3 The traveller Colin Thubron, writing about his experiences in the Soviet Union, recounts the power of brief meetings with people throughout his time there (*Among the Russians*, Heinemann, 1983). He meets Julian at the start of the Iran–Iraq war, near Yalta. 'As we said goodbye, he clasped my hand and said: "if in some future time I see you in the sights of my rifle – I'll miss." "And I won't fire at all,"' Thubron replies, and they laugh. But both are moved by what separated and joined them.

In discussion groups, consider what human qualities and attitudes, hopes and fears, may be common to people the world over. Think about what you have read, what you have learnt about on news and documentary programmes on television, and anything you have actually experienced.

The First Contest

1 'Seeing, looking at what others cannot bear to see, is what my life as a war reporter is all about . . .' writes McCullin in the first chapter of his book.

> Often in battle you think tomorrow it will be you, that you are going to be the one lying with your face to the stars . . . when men have died in front of you, and behind you, there is an overwhelming sense of them dying for you. . . Yet, I ask myself, what has all my looking and probing done for these people, or for anyone? How many times, as the fire was closing on my position, have I thought – Is this it? Is this the day? What have I done with my life?

Explain how his experiences in Cyprus changed him.

2 Discuss what a war photographer does for us that a correspondent doesn't. Is committing yourself to this job a worthwhile way to spend your life?

3 Travel for such a purpose is wholly different from travelling for pleasure. What other work can you think of that involves travel, and what would interest you? After thinking about this, write a short story about yourself in this job.

Desert Rains

1 In the desert, it is possible to experience the discomforts of great heat and bitter cold, the pain of thirst and the chilly saturation of endless rains. What do you think inspires someone like Wilfred Thesiger to travel there?

a) Imagine that you are a reporter greeting him after the journey described in this extract. What questions would you like to ask him? Write down as many as you can think of, and then choose the three best.

b) Try to put yourself in his shoes and answer them.

2 How would you cope if you were a member of Thesiger's team of explorers? Work out what qualities he might look for in you, if he were interviewing you, and honestly assess yourself.

Experiences of a Pioneer Arizona Woman

1 Looking at past events through women's eyes and women's source materials (letters, diaries, memoirs, etc.) gives us fresh and quite different insights into American history. These documents are rich in evidence concerning personal attitudes and day-to-day existence on the Western frontiers. Behind the popular images of men with guns, fighting savages, gambling and drinking hard, we learn about women and men facing westwards with apprehension and loss, working resolutely and bravely for a peaceful life with their children.

Note down the details of Sarah Butler York's journeys that strike you as being almost certainly a woman's concerns and perceptions.

2 Write an imaginative account of a day in the life of Sarah Butler York, taking any detail in her narrative as your starting point.

3 We get a sense of the difference between Sarah Butler York and her husband when she describes his impatience with her uneasiness if he were late coming home after riding after the cattle. Write his version of his day's duties.

4 At a time in history when women were supposed to be passive, obedient, pious and pure, the pioneer women needed different qualities if they were to support their husbands, keep their children safe, and survive themselves. Write a short play in which a man comes to respect his wife for her spirit and independence.

Anger in Saigon

1 James Fenton acts speedily when he sees the child is ill, and takes control. In what ways does he then find himself to be helpless? Note down some examples of how things go wrong, and alongside them suggest what he had expected to happen. Then sum up in your own words the great gap between his expectations and his experience of life in Saigon.

2 He ends by saying: 'It was impossible in Saigon to be the passive observer. Saigon cast you, inevitably, into the role of the American.' What does Fenton mean here? Write down your thoughts.

3 The history of the relationship between Vietnam and America is scarred by war. Find out how they became interlocked, how the war developed, and how the two countries stand now in relation to one another.

On the Way to Pretoria

1 If you were sitting by Gandhi, as a fellow passenger or a friend of his, how would you have felt and reacted when the train reached Maritzburg? Describe the scene as if you had been there.

2 Gandhi's writing style is simple and unemotional, although he describes events that are complex and dispiriting. He presses for justice and at the same time defuses the heat of the situations he finds himself in.

Take one of the exchanges he recounts and rewrite it with a sense of anger on his part. See how differently it might develop if he adopted another style.

3 How do you think you would have responded?

4 Write a description of South Africa at the end of the nineteenth century, based on what Gandhi tells us in this extract from his autobiography, in the form of a letter to a friend contemplating travelling to join you there.

The Crocodile's Bite

1 Only the boys in this society take part in this ritual.
Despite its pain, or perhaps because it is painful, they
are eager to go through it. Even the youngest, who is
afraid, is ready. Explain its significance from their point of
view.

2 As a woman, Christina Dodwell is honoured by their
willingness to initiate her. It is intended as an honour; they
don't do this with their own women.

   a) How do you think she appears to them? Write about her
appearance in the village as if you are one of them.

   b) What would you say or do if this honour was offered to
you?

3 All cultures have ways of making their young people feel
that they are moving from childhood into adulthood. Write
about your own experience of this process. You might be
able to think of particular things that happen, or of things
that are said to you that indicate you are generally thought
of as being older.

The Hopi Snake Dance

1 The Mexican novelist Carlos Fuentes said, 'Mexico is a country far more intricate and challenging to the North American mind than anything in Europe; a country at times more foreign than anything in Asia.'

a) What do you know, or what can you find out, about the differences between these two cultures that share a border, and how might these differences pose problems for both peoples?

b) Do you know of any other two very different countries that share a border? Share your knowledge or the results of your research with the rest of the class.

2 Have you ever seen or held a snake? What might be strange and/or mesmerising about this festival? Explain what would have most captured your attention if you had been there. Perhaps you have had a similar experience that you could recount.

3 What sense do you get of Lawrence's presence in this extract? He wrote himself, at the start of the book:

> We talk so grandly, in capital letters, about Mornings in Mexico. All it amounts to is one little individual looking at a bit of sky and trees, then looking down at the page of his exercise book. It is a pity we don't always remember this. When books come out with grand titles . . . it's a pity we don't immediately visualise a thin or a fat person, in a chair or in a bed, dictating . . . or making little marks on paper with a fountain pen.

We call this presence of the writer in the writing, the 'authorial voice'. In which of the extracts in this book do you get a particularly strong sense of the writer at work, keen to communicate her or his thoughts and feelings?

Overview

1 James Fenton went with Redmond O'Hanlon to Borneo and almost drowned (*Into the Heart of Borneo*, Salamander Press, 1984). O'Hanlon's descriptions are hilarious, but when he asked Fenton to try another expedition together, Fenton dryly responded, 'I would not come with you to High Wycombe,' thinking enough was enough. If you could choose a travelling companion from all the writers in this book, which one would it be? Explain why.

2 In groups, discuss which one of these writers you would most like to meet.

3 Wilfred Thesiger wrote in *Arabian Sands*, 'It is not the goal but the way there that matters, and the harder the way the more worthwhile the journey.' Do you agree?

4 Some people think that travel is much safer nowadays. Maps are more detailed, and methods of transport and the technology linking travellers with outside help have improved. But is this the whole story? What dangers may still exist?

5 Paul Theroux said that the worst trips make the best reading. Is this always so? Look back at the accounts in this book and decide which you personally enjoyed most.

The travellers

Bill Bryson (1951–   ) was born in Des Moines, Iowa. 'Somebody had to,' he once wrote, and 'hardly anyone leaves.' He did, settling in England in 1977, and he now lives with his wife and children in North Yorkshire. One of his books is *The Lost Continent*, a tour of America which has been called 'the funniest book for years'.

Christina Dodwell (1951–   ) lives in London. She has been described as 'a natural nomad' and as possessing 'an insatiable wanderlust'. She has become famous for her lone journeys, sometimes on horseback, in places such as Africa, Turkey and Iran. Two accounts of her many travels are in *A Traveller on Horseback* and *A Traveller in China*.

James Fenton (1949–   ) studied at Oxford, near where he now lives. As a journalist he has worked for a variety of newspapers as a political columnist, theatre critic, book reviewer and foreign correspondent. In 1973–5 he worked as a freelance correspondent in Indo-China. He is also highly regarded for his poetry and was elected Professor of Poetry at Oxford in 1994.

Mohandas Karamchand Gandhi (1869–1948), also known as Mahatma Gandhi ('Mahatma' means 'great-souled'), is regarded by many as the father of his country. He was born in Porbandar, India, and following law studies in England he went to South Africa. After a series of challenges to the government there, he was jailed, and later led the Nationalist movement against British rule in India. He was esteemed for his doctrine of non-violent

protest to achieve political and social progress. His
assassination caused mourning all over the world.

Mary Kingsley (1862–1900) was born in London. At thirty,
after her parents' deaths, she found herself beholden to no
one and in possession of a small income. 'I, out of my life in
books, found something to do.' She went off to West
Africa, 'proceeding on the even tenor of my way, doing
odd jobs and trying to understand things, pursuing
knowledge under difficulties with unbroken devotion'. She
died in South Africa of enteric fever, caught while nursing
Boer prisoners of war.

D. H. Lawrence (1885–1930) was a famous novelist, short
story writer, poet and travel writer. He was born in
Nottinghamshire and made his name with *Sons and Lovers*
(1913), a semi-autobiographical novel set in a poor
Northern mining village. Throughout a lifetime of travel,
especially in Italy, Mexico, Sri Lanka and Australia, he wrote
his other great novels, *The Rainbow*, *Women in Love* and
Lady Chatterley's Lover.

Don McCullin (1935–   ) is a freelance photojournalist. He
left art school in London at fourteen after his father's death.
In 1964 he was sent to Cyprus on his first war assignment
for the *Observer* newspaper; the pictures won him the
World Press Photo Award. Since then he has worked all
over the world and in many war zones, including Vietnam
and Lebanon. He has twice been photographer of the year
and was made a CBE in 1993.

Michelle MacGrath (1953–   ) was born in Southampton.
She has a PhD in Russian literature and spent three years in
Russia studying and working as a translator and style editor.
She currently works with children with specific learning
difficulties (dyslexia) and runs courses in communication

skills, stress management and self-defence. She lives in London and writes poetry and children's books.

Ejnar Mikkelsen (1880–1971) was a Danish explorer and writer. He went to sea at the age of fourteen, and at sixteen he walked 320 miles from Stockholm to Göteborg hoping vainly to take part in an Arctic balloon flight. His most notable expedition was the one he led to north-east Greenland (1909–12). He and Iver Iversen survived two winters in Greenland before they were rescued. He later served as inspector general for east Greenland.

Lynn Pan was born in Shanghai and has lived as an immigrant in North Borneo and England. She has worked as a social scientist, journalist and writer in London, Geneva, Helsinki and Hong Kong, and is especially interested in exploring and documenting the experiences of Chinese people who have a strong sense of their cultural identity and who are far from home.

Helen Sharman (1963–) was born in Sheffield and went to school and university there, graduating with a BSc in Chemistry in 1984. She worked firstly as an engineer and then as a research technologist, suddenly one day hearing on her car radio: 'Astronaut wanted. No experience necessary.' She applied! Since her return from space in 1991 she has continued working as a scientist and now also gives lectures and broadcasts all over the country. She was awarded the OBE in 1992.

Freya Stark (1893–1993) was born in Paris, and was carried over the Alps in a basket two and a half years later. By five, she could speak five languages. At different times in her life she was a nurse and an Arabic scholar, and in World War II she worked for the Ministry of Information in Aden, Cairo, Baghdad, the USA and India. She recorded her love of travel in more than thirty books, and is one of the great travellers of our time, writing fascinatingly and also tenderly about the 'living space of other human souls'.

Paul Theroux (1941–   ) was born in Massachusetts and has travelled through Asia, Africa, North and South America, Europe and the Middle East. His journeys – such as riding trains through Patagonia, sailing down the Yangtze in a junk – are recorded in many books, including *The Great Railway Bazaar* and *Riding the Iron Rooster*. He is also a prize-winning novelist.

Wilfred Thesiger (1910–   ) is a legendary figure: an explorer, writer and soldier. He was the first British child born in Abyssinia (now Ethiopia). *Arabian Sands* and *The Marsh Arabs* are two of his most famous works, recording the way of life of tribal Arabs that has now almost vanished. He has been awarded many medals and awards – the Founder's Medal of the Royal Geographical Society, for example – and he now lives mostly among the pastoral Samburu tribe in northern Kenya.

William Wordsworth (1770–1850), one of our greatest poets, was born in Cumbria. He studied at Cambridge and then travelled in Europe, falling in love with a French girl by whom he fathered a daughter. After his return to England he married Mary Hutchinson and thereafter lived with her (they had five children) and his sister, Dorothy, whose journals and letters give us a view of his life. In 1843 he was made Poet Laureate. He is buried at Grasmere, whose scenery was the inspiration for much of his poetry.

Sarah Butler York. We know little more of this pioneer woman's life other than that which emerges from her account here. Such women wrote diaries and letters but their testimonies to the hardness and adventures of their lives have been overshadowed by the popular view that pioneering was a man's life. The truth is, they were in it together. As one woman staunchly put it: 'We were married to live together, and I am willing to go with you to any part of God's footstool where you think you can do the best, and under these circumstances you have no right to go where I cannot.'

Further reading

The Blessings of a Good Thick Skirt by Mary Russell (Collins, 1986)
These are accounts of the lives of several women travellers who defied the conventions of their times and set off, often alone, to places in the world which were completely unknown to them.

Wayward Women: A Guide to Women Travellers by Jane Robinson (Oxford University Press, 1990)
Here are sixteen centuries of women's travel, with information about each woman's experiences and their written accounts in roughly page-long entries.

Older Than Time by Allegra Taylor (Aquarian/Thorsons, 1993)
Allegra Taylor went on a journey to discover some of the places in the world in which the wisdom of elderly women is important and often central to the happiness of the societies in which they live. It is also a personal journey, as she remembers her own mother and grandmothers.

A History of the World in $10\frac{1}{2}$ Chapters by Julian Barnes (Cape, 1989)
This is a novel, but in Chapter 7, 'Three Simple Stories', the third story is an account of a particular voyage of the liner *St Louis*. It left Hamburg at 8 p.m. on Saturday 13 May 1939, taking Jewish people to safety from Hitler's Germany. You can read about what happened to them.

To Give Them Light: The Legacy of Roman Vishniac edited by Marion Wiesel (Viking, 1993)
If you would like to know more about what those people in the book above left behind them when they boarded the

liner, take a look at this book. Roman Vishniac was a photographer who was born in Russia in 1897 and died in New York in 1990. This book contains his photographs of 'the lost world' of Eastern European Jewish communities, which the Preface describes as 'taking us on an unforgettable journey; from Bratislava to Mukachev and the Carpathians . . . on through the distinct and irreplaceable communities of Poland in Warsaw and Lodz, Lublin and Cracow . . . We meet Jews in those last minutes before they were torn from history by a tempest of fire and ashes.'

The Titanic by Wyn Craig Wade (Weidenfeld and Nicolson, 1979)
This book recreates the events of the night that the *Titanic* sunk and the proceedings of the US Senate investigation.

The Darkness Crumbles: Dispatches from the Barricades by John Simpson (Hutchinson, 1992)
John Simpson is the BBC Foreign Affairs Editor and these are his eyewitness accounts of the fall of Communism in Eastern Europe and the Soviet Union.

Riding the Iron Rooster by Paul Theroux (Hamish Hamilton, 1988)
This famous travel writer describes his journey by rail from London to Mongolia.

The Armchair Traveler: The Best of Travel Writing edited by John Thorn and David Reuther (Prentice Hall Press, 1988)
Some of the best travel writers in the world contribute their experiences: Jan Morris, Jonathan Raban, Colin Thubron . . .

Pearson Education Limited
Edinburgh Gate, Harlow,
Essex CM20 2JE, England
and Associated Companies throughout the world.

This educational edition first published in 1996
Fifth impression 2000

Editorial material set in 10/12.5 point Stone Sans
Printed in Singapore (KHL)

ISBN 0 582 25386 1

Cover by Ship

The Publisher's policy is to use paper manufactured from
sustainable forests.

Acknowledgements

We are grateful to the following for permission to reproduce copyright material:

BBC Worldwide Ltd for an extract from 'The Sepik and the Waghi' by Christina Dodwell in *River Journeys*, publ. 1984 by BBC Books; the author, Bill Bryson for an extract from *Neither Here Nor There* publ. 1991 by Martin Secker & Warburg; the author's agent for an extract from *All the Wrong Places* by James Fenton, publ. 1989 by Viking; Victor Gollancz Ltd for an extract from *Seize the Moment* by Helen Sharman, publ. 1993 by Gollancz; the author, Michelle MacGrath for an extract from the journal *Britain–USSR* No. 64, 1983; Navajivan Trust for an extract from *An Autobiography: The Story of My Experiments with Truth* by Mohandas Gandhi, publ. 1982 by Penguin Books. © 1927, Navajivan Trust; Roman House UK Ltd for an extract from *Unreasonable Behaviour: An Autobiography* by Don McCullin, publ. 1992 by Vintage, 1st publ. 1990 Jonathan Cape Ltd; Reed International for an extract from *Tracing it Home: Journeys Around a Chinese Family* by Lynn Pan, publ. 1993 by Manderin, 1st publ. 1992 by Martin Secker & Warburg; the author's agent for part of 'Subterranean Gothic' by Paul Theroux from *The Best of Granta Travel*, publ. 1991 Granta Publications; the author's agent for an extract from *Arabian Sands* by Wilfred Thesiger, publ. 1964 by Penguin Books, 1st publ. 1959 by Longman Group Ltd. Copyright © Wilfred Thesiger.

We have unfortunately been unable to trace the copyright holders of 'The Liners' by Terry Coleman; *Two Against the Ice* by Ejnar Mikkelson; *Travellers's Prelude* by Freya Stark, and would appreciate any information which would enable us to do so.